## Twelve Proven Steps to Make Your Dreams Come True

Kenn Renner

ISBN-13 978-1466468825
ISBN-10 1466468823

Copyright © 2011 by Kenn Renner
Printed in the United States of America

No part of this publication may be reproduced, stored in a retrieval system, or transmitted in any form by any means – electronic, mechanical, digital photocopy, recording, or any other without the prior permission of the author.

All rights reserved solely by the author. The author guarantees all contents are original and do not infringe upon the legal rights of any other person or work. No part of this book may be reproduced without the permission of the author. The views expressed in this book are not necessarily those of the publisher.

www.PowerGoalsBook.com

## *What People Are Saying About* <u>Power Goals</u>

"I've known Kenn for a long time now and I can tell you this, he lives what he's written about in <u>Power Goals</u>. He's honest, hard working, committed to his family, super creative and one of the top producing sales professionals in Texas. Find out how he does it in <u>Power Goals</u>."

Rob Hutton
President, DR Horton Homes

"Kenn has brought a holistic approach to reaching your goals by incorporating mind and soul into what others have only listed as 'to-dos.' This clear and direct manual reads much like a motivational book, leaving you inspired to achieve your dreams and equipped with the tools to actually do it!"

Danny Thompson
Director of Publishing
Keller Williams International

"If you need clarity and inspiration to achieve the boldest goals, Kenn's book will provide you with a path to a place most people will never dare to visit."

Ben Kinney
Vice President, Keller Williams Technology

www.PowerGoalsBook.com

"Kenn is both my friend and business partner. The insights he shares are practical and transforming when applied to your life. What's more he lives what he writes. He is not a theorist he is a PRACTICIONER. It doesn't get better than that!"

Dr. Raymond Larson
President, 7 Degrees

"As entrepreneurs, we have a tendency to run out of time before we run out of opportunities. Kenn's book Power Goals will help you sort through the clutter to see and seize your best opportunities."

Wesley Young
President, Wes Young & Associates

"Kenn's system is simple, concise, and easy to follow. A model that anyone can use for any goal they want to achieve. Brilliant."

Kenton Brown
Vice President, Sente Mortgage

"Kenn's book is a pleasure to read, he makes goal setting easy with his step-by-step assignments and worksheets are clear and easy to follow. A fast and informative read!"

Debbie De Grote
Maps Master Productivity Coach

"Kenn Renner has an incredible 12-point approach to goal setting that exceeds anything I've ever seen. It taps the emotional, visionary nerves as well as the practical step-by-step procedure. You will achieve or supersede your goals with his formula. I read anything Kenn Renner writes!"

Scott Carley, Motivational Speaker and Coach

"Kenn's book <u>Power Goals</u>, puts into a few pages a lifetime of wisdom and knowledge that everyone should have if they truly want to be successful in life. That success could be anything from getting ahead in the job you now hold, starting a company, or finding the peace that often escapes those on the go. The action steps in your book will enable readers to plan for their success!"

Rick Ebert
President, ALPS

"Kenn Renner's <u>Power Goals</u> incorporates all that one needs to know to not only be successful in business, but also in life. Kenn draws an easy-to-follow blueprint and then it's up to the reader to build upon these powerful parameters of success. <u>Power Goals</u> is both a guide and a workbook that shows what is needed, and what it takes, to change your life."

Mark Loper
Author/Newspaper Columnist

www.PowerGoalsBook.com

www.PowerGoalsBook.com

# Table of Contents

| | |
|---|---|
| Acknowledgements | i |
| Foreword | ix |
| | |
| Introduction to Goal Setting | 1 |
|     Goal Setting | 1 |
|     Standard Setting | 4 |
|     100% Responsibility | 5 |
|     Become a Three Percenter | 6 |
|     The Twelve Steps | 7 |
|     Goals Journal | 7 |
| | |
| Chapter I – Step One – Want | 9 |
| ***Desire / Decide / Commit*** | |
|     Desire | 9 |
|     Decide | 11 |
|         Deciding is Igniting | |
|     Commit | 12 |
|         Commit and never quit | |
|     Action Exercise | 15 |
| | |
| Chapter II – Step Two – Know | 21 |
| ***Believe / Faith / Know*** | |
|     Believe | 21 |
|     Faith | 24 |
|     Know | 27 |
|     Action Exercise | 29 |
| | |
| Chapter III – Step Three – Ink | 31 |
| ***Write It / Speak It / Proclaim It*** | |
|     Write It | 31 |
|     Speak It | 33 |
|         Affirmations | 34 |
|         Reinforcement | 36 |
|     Proclaim It | 37 |
|     Action Exercise | 39 |

## Chapter IV – Step Four – Motives ... 41
### *List Benefits / List Consequences / Motivations*
    List Benefits ... 41
    List Consequences ... 43
    Motivations ... 44
        Get Uncomfortable ... 45
    Action Exercise ... 47

## Chapter V – Step Five – Boundaries ... 49
### *Analyze Starting Point / Define Completion / Boundaries*
    Analyze Starting Point ... 49
    Define Completion ... 51
        Mission Statement ... 52
        Vision Statement ... 53
    Boundaries ... 54
    Action Exercise ... 56

## Chapter VI – Step Six – Time ... 57
### *Set a Deadline / Set a Starting Date / The Stopwatch*
    Set a Deadline ... 57
    Set a Starting Date ... 59
    The Stopwatch ... 59
    Action Exercise ... 61

## Chapter VII – Step Seven – Survey ... 63
### *List Obstacles / Identify Opportunities / Survey Territory*
    List Obstacles ... 63
        The Point of No Return ... 64
    Identify Opportunities ... 65
    Survey Territory ... 67
    Action Exercise ... 70

## Chapter VIII – Step Eight – Information ... 71
### *Identify Information / List Resources / Research*
    Identify Information ... 71
    List Resources ... 72
        Intuition ... 74
    Research ... 74
        Windows of Opportunity ... 75
    Action Exercise ... 77

Chapter IX – Step Nine – Advocates ............ 79
***Identify Those Who'll Help / Identify Those to Avoid / Advocacy***
    Identify Those Who'll Help ............ 79
    Identify Those to Avoid ............ 81
    Advocacy ............ 83
        T.E.A.M. ............ 83
    Action Exercise ............ 85

Chapter X – Step Ten – Plan ............ 87
***Make a Plan / Take Action / Activation***
    Make a Plan ............ 87
        Priorities ............ 90
    Take the First Step ............ 91
    Taking your goals into an Action Plan ............ 92
    Activation ............ 93
    Action Exercise ............ 96

Chapter XI – Step Eleven – Consume ............ 99
***Visualize / Emotionalize / Internalize***
    Visualize ............ 99
    Emotionalize ............ 101
    Internalize ............ 104
        Mind, Heart, Gut ............ 105
    Action Exercise ............ 106

Chapter XII – Step Twelve – Power ............ 107
***Persistence / Patience / Prayer***
    Persistence ............ 107
    Patience ............ 109
    Prayer ............ 110
    Action Exercise ............ 114

Review ............ 115

Action Exercises, Consolidated ............ 117

www.PowerGoalsBook.com

www.PowerGoalsBook.com

## Foreword

Fifty years ago, at the tender age of 19 years, I became the youngest Fidelity Union Life Insurance agent. My general agent, a kind and godly man, was my first success coach. He took me under his wing and began to enlarge my view of life and success. At his recommendation, I began to read everything I could find about success. Some of my early inspirations were the writings of the late and legendary Charlie "Tremendous" Jones. Another was the pioneer of success, a world-changer, Zig Ziglar. Little did I dream that there would come a day when I would get to know them both personally as my friends. They didn't build their careers as mere dreamers. Not at all. They were DO-ers!

Some of the greatest things I learned from these men were quite subtle. I watched Zig Ziglar's love for his wife, Jeanie; and Charlie Jones' love for people and for life. I was impressed with the love each of them had for God. I also learned from them that setting specific goals is indispensable if one is to truly succeed; and that setting goals doesn't come naturally. It's something one must learn to do.

Today, many people are struggling to survive. Once a man asked his friend, "What do you do when you reach the end of your rope?" His friend replied, "That's simple. You tie a knot and hold on." I don't know about you. But I've never met a person who was at the end of his or her "proverbial rope" who had even one specific definable goal--other than "to survive." Survival is certainly important. But success is the "elephant" that must be eaten one bite at a time. Wherever you are today, regardless of your education or lack of education; your experience or lack of experience; or the setbacks you've faced in your past, you CAN succeed! The fact that you are holding this book is evidence that there is potential for success deep inside of you that's waiting to be released!

No matter how high an athlete rises, he or she continues to have a personal coach. Who is your success coach today? Charlie Jones is in heaven. He was simply too good for this earth. <smile> Zig Ziglar is phasing out his extraordinary career, yet God continues to provide life coaches and mentors for each generation. One of our finest motivational coaches is my friend, Kenn Renner.

Kenn is a certainly a dreamer—he's a REAL dreamer! But Kenn is far more than a dreamer. Kenn is a doer—a REAL doer! That alone sets him head and shoulders above 98% of the other dreamers I know. I'll go so far as to suggest that if you are content to dream and not to do, this book is not for you.

However if you, like me, are dissatisfied and discontent to merely dream, and want to attract and accomplish more so you can make a bigger difference in this world, then Kenn Renner's Power Goals: Twelve Proven Steps to Make Your Dreams Come True is the key that will unlock your future. Devour this book, begin to take the 12 steps, and be transformed—then become a transformer!

--Eddie & Alice Smith, Bestselling Authors and Writing Coaches

## Introduction to Goal Setting

## Goal Setting

It has been proven that goal setting is the single most powerful way to achieve desired results. More success has been attributed to goal setting than any other method or strategy. Throughout human history, those who have learned to set goals and take purposeful actions towards achieving them are the ones that accomplish their objectives and change the world.

Today more than ever, learning to set goals will determine success. Less than 3% of the world's population has written goals. More than 80% of the wealth of the world is controlled by less than 3% of the population. Is there a correlation between the 3% that have written goals and the majority of wealth being controlled by such a small minority? Most assuredly.

Clearly defined written goals will propel you towards your success. They provide a roadmap and a compass that will guide you to your desired preferred future. With targeted, compelling written goals in hand, you become unstoppable. Then you must take action every day towards reaching your goals. Goals + action = success.

One of the richest and wisest men in history wrote, "Where there is no vision, the people perish." On the other hand where there *is* vision, the people *flourish*.

People, companies, nations perish for lack of goals, direction and vision. On the other hand, they flourish and prosper in an atmosphere of driving goals and consistent action plans. Those with big goals will find themselves leading the way towards big results.

Why do so few people have written goals when they are so vital to success? One reason is that they were never taught. You can have the equivalent of a university degree, sixteen, eighteen years of formal education and not have had one hour of teaching on goal setting. What a shame. One of my goals is to help change that. Goal setting can be learned and can become a lifelong habit.

Another reason people don't set goals is "fear of failure." They feel that if they set goals and don't achieve them they will let themselves or others down. So rather than face the pain of failure, they don't take a chance on setting simple goals much less lofty ones. It is a common problem. Another reason people don't set goals is that they are not really sure what they want. Everyone was born for a purpose. We all need to take the time to determine what that purpose is and decide what it is that we really want to accomplish. If we don't know what we want we don't have a target. Pulling an arrow back on a bow and not knowing the target is an act in futility. Know what you want, what you were created for, and then go for it. Ancient wisdom exhorts us to "know thyself."

Most all success stories are a series of trials and failures. One of the keys to goal achievement is persistence and patience – *a never give up attitude*. As long as you never stop working towards the end result and learn the art of patience you will cross the finish line with perfect timing. Although many success stories seem like the path was easy, the reality is that the path to success is littered with failures and setbacks. Just because there are inevitable failures along the way does not mean that the individual is a failure. It is only when one gives up and quits that the success story is short-circuited and dream never comes to fruition. Setbacks are inevitable. I like the title of John Maxwell's book, you must learn to "Fail Forward." Past failures do not equal future ones. Consider setbacks as education. The past does not equal the future. You can choose to set new goals and start on a new journey at any time.

We have a saying in our family – "Winning is everything." At first it was meant to be a joke, but when I started thinking about it there was truth in the saying. You must always decide to come from a winning attitude. You must want to win because the alternative is losing. Just because you miss the winning shot or come up short in a relay race does not make you a "loser." Winners are still winning even when they suffer setbacks. Failing along the way is part of winning. As a wise man once said, "one thing I do – forgetting what is behind and straining towards what is ahead, I press on towards the goal to win the prize." Winning is an attitude and becomes a winning lifestyle.

## Standard Setting

If goal setting seems a bit overwhelming at first, start with standard setting. It is interesting when you set standards for yourself or your business. For instance, you may have standards for your income or standards for your health and weight. A minimum standard is a goal in disguise and minimum standards change our perspective of what we expect of ourselves.

Standard means to "stand hard." In military terms, it is a flag or banner that is raised to indicate a solid position or stance of an armed force. Setting standards is something we already do either on purpose or by default. If we don't set our own standards, others will do it for us. Falling below minimum standards causes us pain and consequences.

At one time I felt that an income of $5,000 per month was a lofty goal. When I achieved it I had a huge sense of accomplishment and rightly so. Now $5,000 per month would be below my minimum standard, below survival status. My minimum standard is five figures per month. My goals are much higher than that. What once was a lofty goal is well below my current standard. Amazingly, today my activities and results provide a minimum income standard of more than five figures each month. My goal is six & seven figures per month.

So I encourage you to reach for the stars but also set minimum standards. Incrementally increasing your minimum standards create stepping-stones to reach your goals. Set a standard and then systematically raise the standards. What once may have been a lofty goal will become a minimum standard and become the norm.

## 100% Responsibility

In my studies of goal achievement I have found that the underlying key to success is the realization that we are **100%** responsible for our decisions. Although we are not responsible for all the trials that happen to us on our journey, we are responsible for how we respond to trials and successes. We make choices and we are responsible for them. There is a common disease that works against success. It is the disease of blame and entitlement. It is common for people to blame others or "circumstances" for their position. The impoverished will commonly expect the government to take care of them; that they are somehow entitled to the government dole. The bottom line is that "each of us is ultimately responsible for our own lives."

Between blame and entitlement comes "excuses." We all experience the scourge of excuses. There is no excuse for excuses. "It's not my fault!" – maybe yes, maybe no, but don't make excuses. Excuses are weak and we all have used them to justify why we could not do something.

We must take responsibility for our successes (and humbly admit our shortcomings) and realize the power to choose is ours. We can choose to step into our preferred future or cower back to a life of modest mediocrity. Choose the abundant life! Decide that you are not going to be a victim and make the choice to become a victor.

## Become a Three Percenter

According to achievement expert Brian Tracy, only 3% of the population has written goals. My challenge to you is to become a member of the 3% Club - the 3% of the population that has clearly defined written, inspiring, lofty goals and constantly increasing minimum standards.

Once you join the 3% club with written goals, you too will enjoy the incredible power of goal setting. You will experience supernatural results. You will accomplish infinitely more than you can think or imagine. The good news about goal setting is it is a ***learned activity***. Anyone can do it, will you? I was taught goal setting by an audio program many years ago and it changed my life.

It was then reinforced by seminars I attended and books I read. I learned from Jim Rohn, Brian Tracy, Tony Robbins, Jack Canfield, Zig Ziglar, Napoleon Hill, Myles Monroe, the Bible and many other sources that teach goal achievement. I learned it and I still do it today, and now I teach it to others. It is a habit well worth forming and is a lifelong exercise that produces incredible results.

## The Twelve Steps

The 12-step goal setting technique I will be sharing works for both small and big goals – as well as B-HAGs (Big Hairy Audacious Goals). The 12-step strategy works for both personal and business goals. It is effective in the physical, mental, and spiritual realms as well. Although the 12-steps seem like a lot of work to go through, when you make it a habit, it can be done in as little as 10 to 15 minutes. The foundation of the 12-steps strategy is taken from Brian Tracy's audio program "Maximum Achievement." After years of using this method, I felt that more clarification was needed to make Tracy's program even more powerful and effective, so I have broken each of the 12 steps down into 3 components that will greatly enhance the experience and effectiveness of this achievement exercise.

## Goals Journal

Most of the great achievement experts encourage the use of a goals journal to keep their written goals and dreams in one place. I have been keeping goals journals for decades. It's inspiring to look back at my goals journals and see what I was thinking and dreaming "all those years ago." A goals journal helps you track your progress. It is a place to store great ideas - a storehouse of inspiration. I encourage you to keep a goals journal for all of your dreams and projects. At the end of each section in this book is an action exercise and a place to keep your personal notes and resolutions. You can start your journal with these pages or you can start with a separate goals journal. Please do the action exercises. This is for your benefit to help you create your preferred future.

Now let's embark on the journey towards learning how to achieve all of your big and small goals, dreams, and aspirations. The first step is "want."

Watch Video
http://bit.ly/rJsqA3

Chapter I

Step One

Want

Desire / Decide / Commit

The most famous teacher in history simply asked his students, "What do you want?"

Desire

For a goal to come to fruition, it **must** be something you really, really want. Desire for your objective must also be accompanied by intense passion. The biggest achievements come because of an intense burning desire and a "no quit" attitude. When Bill Gates of Microsoft proclaimed that he wanted his product on "every desk in the world" I am sure he was not casual about his desired outcome. His passion and drive overcame the inevitable obstacles that he encountered. Now his products are found on nearly every desk in the world.

The word "desire" comes from the root meaning "of the father." Your desire for your goal is already in you, like a seed, like DNA. Your goal is waiting to be released, to be planted in good soil. What was once an idea in your mental & spiritual DNA is waiting to burst forth and bear fruit. A goal starts as a small strand of un-manifested mental DNA in the mind of its creator (you) where it begins its journey. Your fervent desire for your goal will bring about results much quicker than a wistful wish. You must passionately desire your intended result. Be specific about your goals. The mind works best when given specific instructions. Write goals in the ***present tense***. Add a future deadline even in the present tense. For instance, "I am making $20,000 per month by June 30th" or "I weigh __X__ pounds by December 31st."

A goal attained is a purpose fulfilled. I believe we were created with purpose and purposefulness. We are here to fulfill a desire. To solve a problem. To perpetuate and to live, love and grow in the purposes we were designed to fulfill. What do you passionately desire? Ask yourself now – what is it I really, really want? For your family, your relationships, and your business – what do you want with all of your heart? Write it down. At the end of this section, you will be asked to brainstorm all the things you want with no limitations.

## Decide

"Deciding is Igniting"

"There is little responsibility in desiring. There is great responsibility in deciding."

You may want something, but until you "decide" and take action it will remain a whim. The root meaning of the word decide is "to cut off." Once you passionately desire something and **decide** to go for it then you cut off any form of retreat. You must burn the bridges of alternatives behind you. A decision is a turning point – a point of ignition. Once the boosters of NASA's Saturn 5 rockets were fired, there was no turning back, and the only alternative was to reach orbit.

Our decisions determine our future, our destiny. Where you are at today is a direct result of the decisions you have made. Where you are going will be determined by the day-to-day, minute-by-minute decisions that you make.

We make thousands of decisions each day – some consciously but a majority unconsciously. Every conscious decision is a "yes" or a "no." "Yes I will go that way" or "no, I will go another way." With a set of clearly written goals your decisions will automatically gravitate toward the "right way" – towards the destiny you want. Clearly defined well-written goals guide the unconscious mind to "stay within the grooves" and to stay on track. Without written goals, people wander. They float and become subject to other people's goals and objectives rather than their own. This is why the 3% of those who have written goals control 80% of the world's wealth. People line up behind and follow those with goals and plans. Decide today to head toward the dreams and goals that will have the most positive impact on your life. Decide to say "NO" to anything that does not line up with where you have decided to go.

## Commit

*"Commit then never quit."*

You may desire a goal and you may decide that you will go for it, but what seals it is when you commit to it. To commit is "to carry into action deliberately" and "to obligate." Commitment is binding. When you commit to a goal you are in a covenant binding agreement with yourself that is not to be broken.

I have to credit the "commit" addition to this narrative to a gentleman who came to one of my seminars. He had recently sold a printing company and he and his partners netted $40 million from the sale. He had recently gone to work at our local real estate office because he was always fascinated by the real estate business (not because he needed the money). He explained to me that there are plenty of unsuccessful people who desire a goal and even decide it is what they want but never **commit** to it. He told me about many occasions when his company was "up against the wall" nearly to the point of bankruptcy. But because he and his partners' tenacity and commitment they were able to pull through the tough times and eventually made a fortune. As with all parts of this goal setting process, you want to **commit in writing**.

Commitment means there is no alternative but to succeed at accomplishing your goal. When I think of commitment I think of marriage or parenthood. I am fully committed to my wife and kids. I would take a bullet for them. I would never give up on them.

You must commit to achieving your goal because there will always be distractions, objections and conflicts that will try to push you off the path. You must give your goal the respect that you would a close family member. In fact, I have heard people talk about their dream as their "baby." A dream worth living for is a goal worth fighting for. And you may have to take a few bullets along the way. Our great nation was formed into existence through the commitment of our forefathers to have a free nation. It was their commitment to the dream that we are a free nation today. Yes the bullets did fly and many paid the ultimate price. Now **that** is an example of total commitment. Did they say "it would be kind of nice to have a free nation for our children's children, but if it doesn't work out, that's ok too?" No! They committed, they resolved to make us a free nation. As the saying goes, "freedom is not free." Goal achievement is not free either. You must commit up front to pay the full price it will take to get you to your dream. Goals without commitment have no power. Resolve today to commit to your goals. It could be a do or die choice for your dreams to become reality.

Watch Video
http://bit.ly/toufPH

## Action Exercise

## Reflections

Make a list of goals you already have accomplished. It is important to pat yourself on the back for your past successes:

_____
_____
_____
_____
_____

What accomplishments or endeavors are you thankful for and proud of?

_____
_____
_____
_____
_____

Who have you met or become in relationship with that you are thankful for?

_____
_____
_____
_____
_____

What **one** accomplishment or endeavor are you most proud of?

_____
_____
_____
_____

What events had the most positive impact on your life?

_____
_____
_____
_____

If you had to do it all over again, what experiences would you like to re-live again?

_____
_____
_____
_____

## Projection

Now to get your creative ambition juices flowing, answer this question: If you were handed $3 million, tax free, what would you choose to do with your time? What activities would you pursue? How would your day look?

Where would you live? What kind of car would you drive? With whom would you spend your time?

_____
_____
_____
_____
_____

If you had exactly one year to live from today, what would you do with your time? With whom would you spend time? What activities would you pursue?

_____
_____
_____
_____
_____

10-Minute Life Changing Goal Setting Exercise:

Get in a quiet place without distractions. Get a timer or stopwatch. Close your eyes and imagine you had unlimited funds and you were free from any hindering responsibilities. If you could have anything you want in the next three years, what would it be? Now list all things you want for yourself, your family, your community, your finances, relationships you want to have, spiritual desires, and material things. Remember, no limitations – make a list. You have 3 minutes:

1. _____
2. _____

3.  _____
4.  _____
5.  _____
6.  _____
7.  _____
8.  _____
9.  _____
10. _____
11. _____
12. _____
13. _____
14. _____
15. _____
16. _____
17. _____
18. _____
19. _____
20. _____

(If you have more than 20, keep going!)

Now circle the **three** goals that if achieved would have the biggest positive impact on your life. Then out of those three, pick **the one** goal that would have the biggest impact on your life. This is the primary goal that we are going to use throughout the action exercises in this book. You can choose any and all of your goals to work through the exercises, but start with the most important ones first!

You will be amazed that 2/3$^{rd}$ of your 3 year written goals will be accomplished in the first 12 to 18 months. You have begun the journey. Now let's go to work.

## Chapter II

### Step Two – Know

### Believe / Faith / Know

#### Believe

"All things are possible for one who believes."

Belief is a powerful force. Beliefs form reality. We filter our world through our beliefs. When we believe in something it becomes "true" to us. When you believe your goal is achievable your mind goes to work to figure out "how." It is a **mindset**. No matter how big your dream is you must first believe that it is attainable. The root of the word "believe" is "to allow." When you believe in your goal you are allowing it to come to fruition. It was said "all things are possible for one who believes." Belief is consciously receiving in advance what you have committed to. Henry Ford said, "Whether you think you can or you can't, you're right." You must say to yourself, "I believe I will do this, I believe this is for me." What you believe you will receive. If you believe health, happiness, and prosperity are yours through goal achievement, you will receive it.

Believing is mental agreement and acceptance. When you believe in a cause, you **agree** with and accept what it stands for. When you believe in your own goals and dreams, you accept them as "yours" – you have rights to them. Belief is our mental frame. It molds our stream of thought and shapes our decisions. At times we may need a renewing of our beliefs. We must cast off beliefs like "I can't," or "I am not worthy," or "I am too old," or "I am too young." Ultimately you are the result of what you believe you can be, do, or have. At goal setting times you must renew your mind. In fact, at goal setting times we need to be transformed by the complete **renewing of the mind**. The old paradigms of defeat and unworthiness must be replaced with a new "can do" attitude. Our world is shaped by what we believe. For a goal to become a reality you must believe to your core that it is meant for you. Beliefs shape cultures, religions, and nations. Beliefs are closely tied to your values – what you believe to be important and worthy. What is really important to you and what is not? What are your core values? What causes do you stand for? Your goals must line up with your core values. Pick five core values you deem as very important.

Make sure your goal compliments these core values. You will not work hard for something you don't value. Values are your foundation and your beliefs are the framework that builds the structure of your current and future reality.

Having clear written goals helps mold your "mindset." Mindset is your current belief frame. Our mind believes certain things and rejects others almost automatically based on our mindset. Our renewed goal setting mindset must be "I can," "I will," "I have," and "I am." A good share of our beliefs and mindsets are formed in childhood and for better or for worse, they carry into adulthood. When we were children, we weren't afraid to believe and pretend. But as we exit our youth we somehow lose the freedom to dream and pretend. We take life too seriously and forget that we were originally programmed to enjoy life.

The opposite of belief is doubt and unbelief. These are dream killers. If you seriously doubt that your goal can come true or if you believe you are not worthy, it won't come to pass. Make a decision to silence that little voice in your head that says, "You can't do this. Who are you to think you deserve such success?" Don't listen to it. It is not your voice. It is a voice that has been programmed to keep you in a comfort zone, mediocrity, or even self sabotage. You must quickly ignore that voice and start your own programming vocal habit saying, "I can do it, I can do it, I will do it, I am doing it." Repeat that over and over.

Doubt is inevitable – and usually comes when struggles appear or when you suffer setbacks. Just be aware that setbacks are part of the process. Stand firm in your commitment. Beat back doubt with a baseball bat. Kick it to the curb. Have a "no quit" attitude. This is not about motivation techniques. Motivation strategies are hard to sustain. Having the **character** of a person who chooses to overcome will sustain you through the tough times. A lifestyle of living in the victory mindset will help push you through. Overcoming setbacks builds character and sets you up to conquer even greater things. You must have an attitude that you are not just a warrior but that you are a conqueror. A conqueror takes territory. You will be taking territory when you start achieving greater measures of influence and success. After conquering comes occupation. You occupy the land, the area, the dominion of your dream. You become **more than a conqueror**. You become an occupier.

Faith

"Faith skips over the 'how.'"

Webster's describes faith as "belief not based on logical (mental) proof or material evidence." Faith accepts things as true regardless of what your mind thinks. When you have faith, there is a certainty that what you are seeking will become real. Faith skips over the "how." Faith is "being sure of what you hope for and certain of that which you do not see." Childlike faith eliminates impossibilities. We must accept our goal with childlike faith; then we need to activate our faith. It is activated by prayer and meditation. Any time you ask for something that does not yet exist, you are activating faith. Whether in prayer or day-to-day self-talk, we are asking the unmanifested to become manifested. So we must be very careful what we ask for. We must be very aware of our self-talk. Having faith in what you want (your goals) gives you substance and sustenance that what you hope for will become reality.

When some one says, "I have faith in you," it means a lot. It is deeper than just hearing, "I believe in you." Faith equals trust. When you have faith in your goal you are activating the supernatural. Your faith in yourself and your dream go beyond the natural. Faith reaches into the future and manifests it to you as real. If you lose faith in your goal and dreams you deactivate the supernatural. Faith in a cause or a goal comes easily for some and difficult for others. Because faith is about trusting in something that has yet to manifest it can be hard to see the end from the beginning. Faith allows us the grace to not have everything all figured out. So it brings us peace. Because it skips over the "how." It is sometimes referred to as "blind" faith. There is a good reason for this. If you were made aware at the beginning of your journey all that you would be going through to reach your dream you might not take the first step.

We live by faith every day. When we are driving, we have faith that the oncoming traffic will stay on their side of the road. We have faith that our lights will turn on when we flip the switch. We live by faith whether we like it or not. So when we have faith in our goals and dreams, we are giving permission to ourselves that "it shall be so." Along our journey we have to live by faith and not by sight. I know there are those of you who may read this and say  – "this all sounds good, but if you only knew where I am at...If you only knew the challenges I face...You would understand why I can't... I can't..."  Well, let me encourage you. By 17 years of age, I had nothing. "Nothing." No hope, no future, no money, no possibilities. A dead end life – reaching an early end. At a crucial life or death moment I decided to live by faith and trust that things would get better if I would "only believe." I did and my life changed and now my dreams are continuing to come true. Loving and living life – yes. Is it easy, without struggle? No! Challenging and fulfilling – yes!

Faith is trust springing from the heart. Whatever is in your heart you trust. What is in your heart you value. Ancient wisdom exhorts, "For where your treasure is, your heart will be also." I encourage you to live in a state of confident expectancy that your dreams and goals will come true – to have faith in your highest aspirations. I encourage you to work hard toward your goals because as a famous saying infers – "faith without deeds (work) is dead." Work is definitely part of the equation - hard work. If goal achievement were easy, without sweat and effort, there would be little satisfaction and fulfillment.

The antithesis of faith is fear. While faith makes real what it is not yet seen in a positive sense, fear believes what it does not yet see in a negative context. It's been said that fear stands for False Evidence Appearing Real. So I ask you to fear "not"! Fear is a dream killer. Faith is a dream maker. Stay focused on faith and don't buy into fear. Stay in a state of unwavering faith and faith will carry you through.

Know

"Knowing is a quiet confidence that what you want will come true"

When you believe your goal is worthwhile and valuable and you have faith it will come to pass, you begin to develop a **knowing** that it will come true. Webster's defines to know as "to believe to be true with absolute certainty." When you **know** something to be true, you feel it deep down in your belly – a "gut" feeling. Simply knowing your goal will become reality makes you more at ease. It gives a sense of freedom, peace, and assurance that what you want will come to pass. Just "knowing" that your objective will manifest gives you unparalleled confidence to move forward and make it happen. Those who achieve great things go day-to-day knowing why and what they are striving for. They know it will become reality. It is clear-cut confidence. Knowing gives you the fortitude to make it through the rough spots. Great achievers will tell you they just knew that what they were striving for would happen. It was not a matter of "if" but "when." As it was said so many years ago, "you shall **know** the truth and the truth shall make you free." Freedom however is not free. It takes strategy, planning, activation, work, persistence, and perseverance. Simply **knowing** that your dream will come to pass will make you unstoppable.

In review, belief is in the mind. Belief is a mental exercise that works through logic – if this, then what? Simple cause and effect. Faith is found in the heart. In the realm of feelings and emotions. Much of what we do is because of how it will make us feel. When you mentally tie your goal with how it will make you ultimately feel, you unleash a powerful effect. Bind your logic with your emotions. Say, "I **believe** with all my **heart** that _(Goal)_ will come true." You will convince yourself into this reality. Knowing is a gut thing. When you get your dream down into your gut, it means you have "swallowed" it whole. It becomes part of who you are. It becomes part of your identity.

- Watch Video
  http://bit.ly/rSnyVz

## Action Exercise

From chapter one's goal exercise, take your #1 goal (and the others when you are ready). Put your left index finger on that #1 goal and your right hand on your forehead and say "I have this" or "I am this" and follow with "so be it." Say I believe _(Goal)_ to be true – so be it. Now move your right hand to your heart and repeat, "I have this or I am this, so be it," then to your stomach and repeat it again followed by "so be it." Then open your eyes and say, "I receive it."

www.PowerGoalsBook.com

Chapter III

Step Three – Ink

Write It / Speak It / Proclaim It

Write It

"Write the vision..."

Writing your goals down is probably the single most important step in effective goal setting. A goal that is not written is simply a "wish." An unwritten goal has no power, no weight. Ancient texts tell us to "write the vision. Make it clear on tablets so that anyone can read it quickly. The vision will still happen at the appointed time. It hurries toward its goal." Many top achievers carry their written goals with them. They read them and re-read them. I re-write my goals every time I do my weekly & monthly to-do lists. I suggest that you handwrite your goals. It is remarkable what happens between the brain and the pen. To "write" is "to express & to compose." Hand writing your goals make them more real to you. It is a creative expression. When you handwrite the goal, you see it with your own eyes as it hits the paper. I encourage you to put this entire 12-step goal setting exercise in writing. Written goals help you stay accountable to them. Another reason to have them in writing is so that you can look back at them some time in the future to see what was important to you at any particular season of life. It's fun for me to look back at my goals journals from years past and see what I was striving for. One goal that I had written years ago that I found humorous was "marry Michele," my girlfriend at the time. We have been happily married for nearly two decades. Another one was "I want to be the Anthony Robbins of real estate. Anthony Robbins is a very popular motivational author and speaker. Through the years, I have sold several hundred millions of dollars in real estate as a direct result of my public speaking engagements. Honestly, writing goals becomes fun when you begin to see tangible results from this simple activity.

Back in my early 20s, I was in a popular rock band called "The 5:15 Band." At the time I thought we would head to superstardom but you know the typical story – "the bass player quit" and "the drummer got married…" One of my written goals at the time was to perform "live" in front of 35,000 people. A pretty lofty goal for an unknown band, right? Well, our band was a great vocal group that sang harmonious "a capella" tunes (although I was the keyboard player and the only member of the band that did not sing). We recorded an a capella version of the National Anthem and submitted it to the major league baseball team the Anaheim Angels. And to our delight, they gave us a spot on the schedule to perform the National Anthem at Anaheim Stadium. When we got there it was surreal. Time stood still. Then to stand at home plate and perform our Nation's theme song in front of 35,000 Angel fans was amazing. It was a goal achieved in an almost supernatural way.

What was even more amazing is that I sang the song with the band – even though I was not a "singer." In fact, ***it was the first song I ever sang in public***. Now that is the power of putting goals in writing.

Watch Video
http://bit.ly/sQqMQp

Speak It

Next, speak out your written goal. To speak out is to "talk freely, fearlessly, unhesitatingly." The expressed spoken word carries great creative power. God **said**, "Let there be light and **there was**." You must speak out your goal with confidence and conviction. When you speak out your goal you articulate with your mouth. At the same time your ears receive it with the voice that you are most familiar with – your own. When you speak your goal aloud you are creating an atmosphere of trust & confidence. When you speak your goal, you can taste it. It's on the tip of your tongue. The goal is becoming real by your spoken word. Repetition is also important. Affirm your goal every day – several times a day. When you are driving, when you are working. Affirm with "I am __(Goal)__ because __(Reason)__ so that __(Result)__." There is extensive research and proof that spoken affirmations are powerful and effective. Use affirmations daily – they will change your life.

## Affirmations

Affirmations are short sayings that agree with your desired results. Repetition is the key. Once your mind hears your voice affirm positive desires and outcomes repetitively, it will begin to believe them to be true. Your thoughts and daily actions will line up with your repeated affirmations. I like affirmations to have a rhyme when possible, like: "I am happy and healthy in every way, I am getting better and better every day." Another one I use is "I am easily and consistently closing two million in sales every month." This one doesn't rhyme but when I reach that goal it is music to my pocket book.

Keep in mind that speaking affirmations and results can also be used against you. Most of our thoughts and actions are the results of programming and programming is often by default rather than on purpose. Negative default affirmations are programmed in childhood, often unintentionally by parents and others. We have to be very careful of our speech. What we say to ourselves (and others) has subconscious impact – especially negative words. One of the first words we learn is "no." No gets so overused in our childhood it can translate into paralysis in our adult years. When our inner child says "wouldn't it be great to become _____?" The ***"no"*** in your subconscious can shut you down. Self-talk is so powerful it will determine your destiny. I witnessed this in my own life when my wife would relate a negative situation; she would have a habit of responding with "I feel so bad that this happened…" or "I feel so bad they are in troubled times…" She was just trying to be compassionate but I realized that those four words, "I feel so bad…" started becoming a self-fulfilling prophesy. After saying to her friends "I feel so bad that your mom got sick" or "I feel so bad that you didn't get the job" she literally started feeling bad and at times in a serious way. Our positive self-talk and affirmations have a powerful positive impact on our future; our negative self-talk and affirmations have a negative one. This is not psychobabble – this is reality. The good news is you can re-program negative self-talk with positive, consistent, repetitive affirmations and by speaking your written goals. Take a moment and commit yourself to include positive life giving affirmations into your daily routine. Make it a lifestyle. It will change your life – really!

## Reinforcement

It is important to speak out your written goals on a daily or at least weekly basis. Simply take out your goals journal and read them aloud with confidence and conviction. Don't use words like "try" or "might." Your mind says, "Trying is lying." You must constantly reinforce the goal you are seeking. Whether or not it seems like it is coming to pass as expected is not the concern. The objective is that you are speaking your desired positive results with conviction. Conviction means "convinced." Are you convinced that your goal is worthy of pursuit? Then speak it out on a regular basis. Your subconscious will go to work to align with the spoken commands. Where do you speak these goals and affirmations? In front of a mirror is great. When you are driving. When no one is around so you can speak loudly with convincing proof to yourself that your dream will come to pass. Sometimes I am reviewing my goals in a crowded restaurant. Not the most convenient place to speak out lofty goals. What I have found is that speaking goals and affirmations low and almost inaudible can also be effective. It's kind of like when your kids are out of control and you are finished trying to convince them to do what you want them with your louder voice. It can be very effective to kneel down in front of them, look them straight in the eyes, and with a quiet but firm voice let them know your desired result. At that point I know my kids get the point. So use those times when you can't speak out loudly and speak your goals and affirmations to yourself like a serious parent on the edge of implementing discipline.

## Proclaim It

*"...For out of the heart, the mouth speaks."*

Once you have written your goal and spoken it aloud repetitively, you need to proclaim the goal. Proclaim is to "claim in advance." When you claim something, you are calling it your own. You are taking possession of something that you already own. Like claiming an inheritance that is rightfully yours. All you have to do is step up and claim it. When you proclaim that your goal is to have "X" amount of income or "X" body weight, you are claiming it in advance. Proclaiming is a shouted declaration. To declare is to "make known formally & officially." Declaring your goal is setting it in stone and proclaiming it lets all hear that it is to be.

Think about how powerful and effective the "Declaration" of Independence or the Emancipation "Proclamation" was when announced by our Nation's leaders. The signers of the Declaration of Independence risked everything for what they believed. Many were wealthy businessmen and landowners. By signing the Declaration they were telling the King of England, "Our goal of independence is do or die." They knew if they lost the fight they would lose everything and quite possibly pay the ultimate price. When Lincoln signed and read aloud the Emancipation Proclamation, he was putting his political career and the future of the Nation in consequence for the goal of freedom for all men. We need to have the same conviction regarding our important life changing goals and proclaim them aloud and even in public. When I made it a goal to write this book, I made a proclamation to my wife, family, friends, co-workers. I proclaimed it at the seminars I was teaching. I just had to "shout it out loud." Proclaiming it also keeps us accountable. I would have many people (even those I didn't know) say to me, "How's the book coming?" Proclaim your goals aloud and with conviction to the important goal-oriented people in your life.

Watch Video
http://bit.ly/rs7Qmg

## Action Exercise

Take your important goals from the chapter one exercise and fill in these sentences – put the goal in present tense (as completed):

I am

_____
                      (Identity / Existence)

Because

_____
                      (Reason / Cause)

So that

_____
                      (Results / Effect)

Example:    I am <u>earning twenty thousand per month every month by June</u>
Because <u>I have children going to college and I want a nicer home</u>
So that <u>I am comfortably providing for my family's security and college education.</u>

Repeat this exercise with all your important goals and keep them in your goals journal. Put the statements in a place you can see them daily. On your bathroom mirror, a white board at your office, or on the visor of your car.

www.PowerGoalsBook.com

## Chapter IV

### Step Four – Motives

### List Benefits / List Consequences / Motivations

### List Benefits

### "For the Joy Set Before Me…"

You need to recognize the benefits you expect to enjoy as a result of achieving your goal. Benefits are the rewards for your efforts. How will achieving your goal make you feel? What new opportunities will it open up for you?

Attach emotions to the future benefits. Close your eyes and imagine the future benefits unfold. Put a big smile on your face (or for that matter, laugh out loud). The more benefits, the more likely you will want to achieve it. Think of the rewards big and small that you expect to receive. Imagine yourself being the beneficiary of the results of your goal achieved.

Benefits are related to the word "beneficiary." A beneficiary implies inheritance. When you list your benefits you are describing your inheritance. We would expect an inheritance to help make our lives easier. Ease some financial burdens or allow us a greater measure of freedom. So take your inheritance seriously and list all the good things that will result from your goal as accomplished. Have fun with your benefits list. If it benefits you it will most likely benefit someone else. List others who will benefit as well. "I have my children's college education paid for by (date)." List the benefits for you "and" your child.

Recognizing the benefits of a goal achieved will help motivate you towards its completion. When you realize how many other people will benefit from your efforts it gives you a sense of purpose beyond your own personal ambitions. When things get tough and you lose sight along the way, pull out your benefits list and review the motivating reasons that you are striving for. Take time periodically and review your benefits list. It will help you get through the tougher times when you say to yourself "Ok, so why am I doing this?" Then pull out your goals journal and review the multitude of benefits your goal achieved will provide. Fun stuff!

If earning a million dollars in a year is your goal, write down what that would do for you, your family, your church & charities? If owning a beautiful beachfront condo in Hawaii is your goal, what would that do for you? Make a list:

1. A place to recharge
2. A place to bond with my family on vacation
3. A place I can leave to my children or grand children when I pass.
4. A good investment for future appreciation or income
   and on and on…

## List Consequences

The next step is to consider the consequences of what might happen if your goal is not achieved. What would you miss out on? Imagine yourself turning 80 years old and looking back you say, "If I only woulda, or I wished I coulda." Now bring it into the present and say, "If I don't take this action now, I will end up like this _____?_____…" If your goal is to stop smoking, list the future consequences of not doing so. My mother smoked two packs a day and died in her early 40s. The consequence is that we don't get to share the wonderful moments of our lives with her. I don't want to spend too much time on the negative but the future consequence of a dream not achieved could very well be the catalyst to get you motivated. Pain of loss is a greater motivator than the pleasure of gain. Attaching painful results to "not" reaching your goal will spur you on to your preferred future.

So many times we make seemingly insignificant decisions that don't align with our preferred future and as a result we end up way off course. Our written goals and plans will help us **choose right**. We do have the power of choice – the power to choose both big and small decisions. We have free will. If we knew the results of many of our choices ahead of time we would never choose them. Become a consequence-aware person. Every choice we make has short and long term results. I can't tell you how many versions of A Christmas Carol I have read or watched, but the moral of the story is one we need to take to heart. Scrooge was a transformed man once he saw the future results of his past choices. We can be transformed when we acknowledge the list of consequences of our goals "not achieved."

Motivations

The benefits and consequences are your motivating factors. To motivate is to "get moving," to put in motion. For motivation to be sustained you need to constantly remind yourself of the benefits and consequences. Get an accountability partner or achievement coach who will continue to encourage you and hold your feet to the benefits & consequence fire. Motivational seminars are great but their effectiveness fades quickly. Find or hire someone you trust to help you stay motivated and moving forward. Post your goals and the list of benefits on your mirror. Put them on your screen saver. I shared this strategy at the dinner table one night with my family. My son, Justin, took my advice. He was on the freshman basketball team and he had made only four points his previous game. He then made it his goal to make twenty points. In a few days, they were going to play the same team that they had played the previous week. Justin made a list of benefits and consequences of making twenty points. Sure enough, he achieved his goal of hitting twenty points – it's on video on his YouTube channel. Needless to say, Justin became a believer in the motivational power of goal setting and listing benefits.

Watch Video
http://bit.ly/s5LKyc

Get Uncomfortable

We all have a tendency to revert to complacency – to what is comfortable. You *must* become uncomfortable with being comfortable. To expand and stretch yourself involves some effort and some pain. Ask anyone who hires a trainer to become physically fit. The trainer pushes their clients beyond what is comfortable and the majority of results come from the last few repetitions of the exercise.

A "motive" is the underlying reason for someone's actions. Your underlying motive is tied directly to what you expect your reward to be – your big "why". When you habitually review your desired results and motivations it will help push you down the track like an energized version of the "Little Train That Could." Repeat to yourself "I know I can, I know I can" (not "I think I can"). True motivation is saying, "I know I can." Goal achievement is a battle. It is a good fight and you must fight for your dream every day! Fighting is rarely comfortable, but it is a requirement. We soon become conquerors. In fact, our job is to become **more than a conqueror**. It is to become an "occupier." Once we have taken the territory of our destiny we then get the privilege to occupy and live in our dream. Our preferred future is worth the "good" fight. So we must get comfortable with being uncomfortable.

Watch Video
http://bit.ly/unJRyN

## Action Exercise

List ten to twenty benefits you or others will expect to enjoy when you reach your goal. The first ten will be easy. It will get more difficult as you get to twenty. Push through - the more benefits you list, the more motivated you will be.

1. _____
2. _____
3. _____
4. _____
5. _____
6. _____
7. _____
8. _____
9. _____
10. _____
11. _____
12. _____
13. _____
14. _____
15. _____
16. _____
17. _____
18. _____
19. _____
20. _____

List five or more serious consequences that will result if you do not reach your goal. Be real. These may be your catalyst for change.

1. _____
2. _____
3. _____
4. _____
5. _____

## Anchoring Exercise

Now close your eyes, think of your goal, and open your hands as if to receive a gift. Say, "I receive the benefits of my goal achieved." Next, put your hands out in front of you as if to push away something you didn't want and say, "I resist the notion of my goal not being achieved. I push away the consequences." Now raise your hands above your head and say, "I reach into the future and pull my goal to me." Then pull your hands down towards your heart as if pulling fruit off of a tree. Then say, "I receive, I believe – so be it."

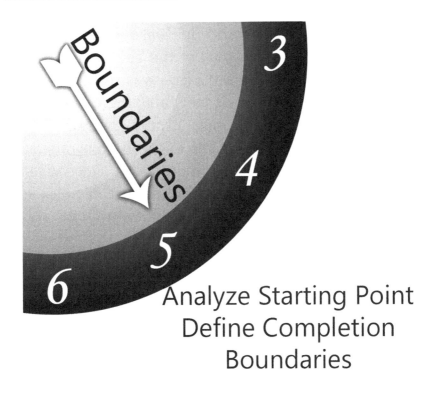

# Analyze Starting Point Define Completion Boundaries

Chapter V

Step Five – Boundaries

Analyze Starting Point / Define Completion / Boundaries

"...Where are you?" - God

Step Five in the goal setting process is to analyze your starting point. To "analyze" is to break something down into its elemental parts. When setting out on a mission or starting a project you must break down and categorize the collateral you have to begin with. Before going on a mountain climbing expedition you must lay out all of your gear to see what you have and what is missing.

I remember when my father would take us on hunting & fishing trips. Before we left, all of the gear would be laid out on the garage floor. Each piece was tested. We had most of what we needed but inevitably there were a few crucial items that were missing. It may have ruined our experience if we had not broken out everything ahead of time to see what we had – or didn't have. Once we saw what was missing we could go buy it or we could pick it up on the way rather than go into the field without it.

Ancient wisdom exhorts, "...but don't begin until you count the cost. For who would begin the construction of a building without first calculating the cost to see if there is enough money to finish it?"

So if your goal is to become financially free, you must begin with analyzing where you are currently at financially. Start with a simple asset & liability statement to show net worth. Then analyze your monthly profit & loss statements to see your income and out go. You must know your starting position – a breakdown of where you currently are at.

You may need to consult with an advisor who can tell you what is missing in your analysis. For many years I was the president of a mortgage company. When I took a loan application from a borrower there would be a checklist of all the items that were needed to complete the loan package. Inevitably there were items missing. I would give my clients the list of the missing documents and they would go home and retrieve them. We could not complete the funding of the loan without all the pieces being in place.

The good news is you may find that you already have more in place than you think. When I made it my goal to earn my real estate broker's license the state required me to have a certain number of college hours in core subjects as well as non-core subjects. When I broke down and analyzed what classes the state required I found that several courses I had taken in college satisfied the state's requirements saving me countless hours of education that I otherwise would have had to complete.

Don't be discouraged if it seems that you don't have the resources at hand. Most all of us start our journeys with limited resources and knowledge. It's OK because you can *learn* what you need, what to do and where to go to gather the resources.

It is important to be honest with yourself about your starting position but certainly don't let humble beginnings hold you back. An ancient proverb encourages us, "do not despise these small beginnings."

## Define Completion

It is important to define what your goal looks like when it is achieved. People often set ambiguous goals that they are never clear about when they have achieved it. "I want to be rich" is not clear. "I have $1 million cash in the bank by age 55" is a clearly defined goal.

When you get on a soccer field and start towards the goal the only time you score (achieve your goal) is when the ball goes into the net. All the fancy moves don't matter – the only thing that matters is that the ball goes into the net. Great satisfaction comes from knowing what you want to achieve then going for it day-by-day, week-by-week, moving towards your target and then knowing when you have hit the mark.

## Mission Statement

The mind, will, and emotions work much better with clear-cut goals and well defined written preferred outcomes. A mission statement helps with defining completion. A mission statement could be: "I am happily helping fifty disadvantaged children in the inner city become successful entrepreneurs through educational and inspirational programs," or "I am helping provide 20 college scholarships per year through government sponsored programs and philanthropic organizations." How will you know your goal is achieved? – When 20 kids are going to college with scholarships.

A mission statement is consise. It needs to be clear, descriptive, and concise. Here is an example:

> The mission of the Big Brothers / Big Sisters of America is to make a positive difference in the lives of children and youth, primarily through a professionally supported, one-to-one relationship with a caring adult, and to

assist them in achieving their highest potential as they grow to become confident, competent, and caring individuals by providing committed volunteers, national leadership, and standards of excellence.

My mission statement is:

Living, loving, and growing in the purposes God has for me and helping others to do the same.

Write a short, powerful, engaging mission statement for each of your important goals.

## Vision Statement

A vision statement is a paragraph or two describing, in detail, the future reality of your completed goal. It describes the emotions and feelings of satisfaction you associate with your goal when it is achieved. It is a snapshot of that future day. Describe who is with you. What are the circumstances surrounding that day? Close your eyes and peer into the future and watch a mental home movie of that day in the near or distant future. Define the completion of each of your goals with a written vision statement. As Stephen Covey states, "begin with the end in mind."

## Boundaries

Along with knowing your starting point and the definition of the completion of your goal, it is important to define the boundaries. The boundary lines define whether you are "in the game." As life would have it, many times we think we are on track to reach a goal and then we go astray. We get distracted. We "foul out." You must know and be clear when you are "in the game" and when you are not. During the process of achieving a goal it is helpful to have a coach or an accountability partner help you stay "in bounds." The field of play in sports is very well defined. At times we may think we are really hitting it hard only to find out that we are missing the mark or "golfing in the wrong fairway." It's like working on a savings plan and then spending way too much. It does no good to save diligently for 12 months and then blow double that amount on a new ski boat and think you are "getting ahead." Believe me – I have been in that "boat" and honestly struggle with staying in the boundaries. We don't always like boundaries but they are there for good reason. To keep us in the playing field. Those that don't want to live within the boundaries are destined to live a life of mediocrity or even potential disaster.

As your influence expands through achieving more and more, you will find your playing fields become bigger and bigger. The competition will get stiffer as you step into new realms of achievement. When your boundaries expand and you exert yourself to the extreme you break through the ranks and head into open (sometimes unknown) territory. Yes, there will be times of setback. Just know that setbacks are not permanent. When you get knocked down, get up, brush yourself off and get moving again. The goal posts are just a few steps away. Staying within the boundaries is a continual practice of reviewing and analyzing your results along the way.

What does the mountain climber see when he gets to the top of the mountain? Yep, more mountains to climb. So guess what happens once you meet your goal? That's right! There is another exciting goal waiting to be achieved. Life is a goal-achieving journey. Make the most of it and enjoy the view. Will there be struggles on the way? Yes. Will there be victory in the end? Yes. Just as long as you never ever give up.

Watch Video
http://bit.ly/stSFLh

## Action Exercise

For each of your goals, write down your current starting position. For instance, if your goal is to have $1 million cash by age 55, write down how much cash you have right now. If you are trying to achieve a certain weight, write down your current weight. Then write out your goal as completed – clearly and concisely.

Where are you currently?

_____

_____

Now clearly define your goal as completed:

_____

_____

# Set a Deadline
# Set a Starting Date
# The Stopwatch

## Chapter VI

### Step Six - Time

Set a Deadline / Set a Starting Date / The Stopwatch

#### Set a Deadline

You must set a deadline for the completion of the goal. All goals must have a written deadline – a specific date. Our subconscious works very well to meet deadlines. Without deadlines, we can succumb to a number of anti-goal achieving activities such as procrastination and distraction. It is easy to put off important things and trade our time for the more menial and even unnecessary activities in our lives. Busyness is a rampant scourge in our society. ***It is very easy to be busy and yet not effective***. You must consciously move away from being busy to becoming effective. Constantly ask yourself, "Is this what I should be doing right now? What is the most effective use of my time right now?"

Deadlines are productivity motivators. Did you ever cram late night for a final exam? How much do you get done the few days prior to leaving on a two-week vacation? Can you imagine how our lives would be if we worked like we were just about to leave on a long vacation? We make lists of things we need, make sure pets are cared for, check things off our list as we get them done. We are very focused as the deadline approaches. We know that plane leaves at a specific time and date – a deadline. Deadlines are good. The world runs by deadlines. Does April 15$^{th}$ ring a bell? Of course it does. Deadlines rule.

So what happens if you don't meet the deadline? Simply set another deadline. Knowing that you can extend the deadline is not an invitation to fall into procrastination. Even writing this book I played the "busyness" card. I missed my first deadline. I set another deadline and I strived to meet that deadline. Why? Because this book will help change lives for the better. And it is not something I take lightly. I was commissioned to write this book and I had a deadline, yet when I didn't meet it, I set another one. A publisher told me recently, "A half written book is no book at all." That was a wake up call for me to get writing and meet my deadline.

## Set a Starting Date

You need to have a deadline and you also need a starting date or a birthing point. Make a commitment and resolve to begin on a certain date – a commencement date. It is all too easy to make plans and goals and then never get started. Write down the starting date and resolve to **take the first solid action on that date**. It could be as simple as picking up the phone and making a call or stepping outside to take that first long healthy walk. Setting a starting date is as important as setting a deadline. I suggest not making your starting date New Year's Day. More resolutions are broken "the day after New Year's" than any other day. How about starting that dream-achieving goal *now*? There is power in "now." "I am starting today" is a very motivating and engaging statement. Set a starting date, then "start." Begin the journey. On that date, review your goals journal. Engage all the "whys." Review why you want what you want. Then pull the trigger and start to run down the track.

## The Stopwatch

Remember the beginning of the show "60 Minutes." There is something intriguing about the visual of the stopwatch and the sound – tick, tick, tick. When you see and hear that watch you know the show has begun and there will be a sixty-minute presentation – tick, tick, tick. Before and after each commercial break is once again that stopwatch reminding us that this is a sixty-minute show. Once you have set a deadline for your goal and decide on a start date, it becomes like that stopwatch. Go! – tick, tick, tick. The stopwatch is neither biased nor lenient. It keeps track of the race we are running. The stopwatch does not lie. It compares our performances to similar past performances or to others who have run the same course.

Once you have begun, take action steps every day towards your goal. Always keep moving towards the preferred future. Don't stop fighting for the cause. Your future or your life may depend on it. Our goals will be achieved because we push past our limit of our current capacity. It reminds me of those cheesy South Western desert postcards I used to see on road trips with the picture of the pioneer skeleton found just inches away from reaching his water canteen. Our victory may just be inches or minutes away. It is common to want to give up at the last minute – don't do it! Press in, press on – your victory may just be a "tick" away.

Watch Video
http://bit.ly/urHpJ9

www.PowerGoalsBook.com

## Action Exercise

Now take your most desired goal and write down a start date:

I will begin _____
                        (goal)
on _____.
                     (start date)

Now write down a deadline. Use a future date in the present tense, Ex. "I weigh __X__ pounds on June 1, 2014":

I_____
                        (goal)
on_____.
                  (completion date)

Now read the goal and the start date and deadline aloud so you hear it for yourself.

# List Obstacles
# Identify Opportunities
# Survey Territory

Chapter VII

Step Seven - Survey

List Obstacles / Identify Opportunities / Survey Territory

List Obstacles

Every journey will come with its share of obstacles. The bigger the goal the greater the obstacles. Don't let obstacles keep you from your dream. Resistance is a healthy and necessary part of any endeavor. When obstacles are defined they become quantifiable, easier to measure and less intimidating. When you identify the obstacles they become smaller in your mind. Identifying the known obstacles will help you begin the "overcoming" process. Fear is a great de-motivator. Fear of the unknown is a killer. It leads to stress and paralysis. Listing the obstacles takes away the fear factor. We see what we need to overcome. The mind goes into action automatically seeking solutions. The question is not "<u>if</u> I will overcome the obstacles," but "<u>how</u> I will overcome the obstacles." The great explorers Lewis & Clark had to find their way across mountain ranges, raging rivers, marshes, and deserts. There was no question of "if" but "how." Do or die. If you attach that kind of passion and commitment to overcoming your obstacles, there is no limit to where you can go.

## The Point of No Return

When Columbus and other Atlantic explorers sailed towards the Americas there was a point where the captain had to make a choice of continuing on to the New World or turning back. That was the point where they had just enough food and supplies to make it back to the European mainland if they turned around. It was called "the point of no return." Talk about courage! There was no guarantee if they continued west that they would reach land. They had to overcome their fear obstacle as well as the other troubles they would encounter. One of those obstacles ahead was called "The Doldrums." The Doldrums occurred in parts of the Atlantic at certain times of the year where the winds just don't blow. There was nothing to fill the sails and push them on to their goal. You will most likely face the Doldrums along your goal-achieving journey. Just realize that the Doldrums are temporary. Don't make any major snap decisions when you are in the Doldrums. Kick back, think of the future, go swimming and pray for the winds of change to blow sooner than later to get you back in motion again. Don't worry – the winds will blow again. They always do.

Obstacles are opportunities for growth and character building. When the mountain blocks your way or the raging river stops your progress, it's time to come up with solutions. It gets your creative brain thinking. At times, the problem may seem insurmountable, but think of Lewis & Clark. They faced it all and overcame. Your persistence in overcoming will help you navigate up & over, through, across or around the obstacles in your way. You'll become stronger, more confident, and more experienced by overcoming.

## Identify Opportunities

Opportunities are all around us – all the time. When you become goal oriented you become an opportunity seeker and an opportunity magnet. I often ask myself when I get started in my day, "what opportunities will I find today that will help improve my life or improve the lives of others?" Make a list of the opportunities you currently know of that will help you meet your goal. The root meaning of the word "opportunity" is "to port." A port is a hub of trade and commerce. Ships come in from distant lands and drop off their cargo. Rail lines and transportation companies bring raw and manufactured goods to the port for passage to other parts of the world.

The ships and crews get re-supplied with fuel and provisions. Ports are filled with new opportunities and possibilities. What goods and services can you trade? What can you bring to port? What will you offer in trade for the things you need? When you are out sailing the high seas all you see is the wide-open ocean. But when you pull into port all kinds of possibilities present themselves. In our business lives ports could be networking meetings, trade shows, industry business conferences, and office meetings. Make a list of great ideas or products that compliment your goals. You might find a problem solving solution in a book or in a presentation or seminar. I met one of my best friends and business partners while visiting a booth at a Home and Garden Show.

Seek opportunities everywhere. Keep your mind open especially if you are short on ideas. Then make sure you select only the best opportunities for your objective. When you become an entrepreneurial goal-oriented individual more and more opportunities will present themselves. Many of them will look good. But as Jim Collins stated, "good is the enemy of great." You will soon get to the point where you have more opportunities than you will have time or money to pursue. You must choose only the **right** opportunities. Otherwise, you will run out of time, money, and energy. Chasing just "OK" or just "kinda cool" ideas can lead you away from greatness.

One opportunity that gets overlooked is being really good at your current core responsibilities. I call it being

***brilliant at the basics***. For example, in my real estate brokerage business, "lead generation" (i.e. calling on prospects) is a core duty. Our team's goal is to lead generate a minimum of three hours per day every working day. Although that sounds like a lot, it is only 15 hours out of a 40 or 50-hour workweek. I admit it's sometimes a struggle meeting that goal, but I know that it is crucial to my business so I make it a priority to hit that three hours a day.

When you start heading toward an objective your attention is drawn towards things you may have normally missed. I remember when it was time to expand my offices I began to see office space signs everywhere. They existed there before but when I started focusing on my goal the signs seemed to pop out everywhere. The same will hold true when you head towards your goal. What you focus on will expand. The signs of opportunity will begin to appear. Just make sure you choose the best ones for you.

## Survey Territory

Next you need to survey the territory into which you are about to move. To survey is to "look over." The territory is the land, region and spheres of influence in an area. You have listed the obstacles and the opportunities. Now take a 10,000-foot view of the territory. Who occupies the land now? Where are the steepest climbs? Is money a challenge for you to proceed? Where on this map will you find sources of funds? I have helped thousands of home buyers become homeowners. It is satisfying to sit down with my clients and talk about the "territory." Not only in terms of where they want to live but also how they are going to get there. Down payment can sometime be a challenge. In one case, my clients were about $1000 short to close on a home purchase. We surveyed their assets and found out that they had inherited a horse (we are in Texas). The horse was worth $1200 and we were able to sell the horse and meet the down payment requirements. They now own a home with money they found by taking a survey of their territory.

If your goal is to become financially independent through investing take a mental survey of "the land." What is the current economic climate? Where are the best locations to invest? What challenges are there in financing that will need to be overcome? Keep in mind that you probably need to engage the services of a coach, guide, or advisor to help quicken your journey. They will already know the terrain and can help. Business coaching is big business – for good reason. Properly executed coaching works.

It is important to review **who** currently occupies the territory as well. For instance, if your goal is to be elected as mayor or to congress you will want to survey the current regime and the potential candidates. What are the spheres of influence in that territory? Who has been successful? Who is corrupt? Who influences the influencers?

www.PowerGoalsBook.com

In ancient days, a leader requested his explorers to: "Look the land over, see what it is like. Assess the people: are they strong or weak? Are there few or many? Observe the land: is it pleasant or harsh? Describe the towns where they live: are they open camps or fortified walls? And the soil: is it fertile or barren? Are there forests?"

Surveying ahead of time will give you a bird's eye view of the territory you are about to conquer.

Watch Video
http://bit.ly/uR9mSF

Action Exercise

List five opportunities that you can think of that currently align with your goal that you can capitalize on:

1. _____
2. _____
3. _____
4. _____
5. _____

Circle the best opportunity for you at this time. Now say out loud, "I will seize this opportunity now."

List the 3 biggest obstacles or fears you have that would hold you back from obtaining your goal.

1. _____
2. _____
3. _____

Now declare out loud these obstacles as small, not significant, and having no power over your destiny.

# Identify Information
# List Resources
# Research

Chapter VIII

Step Eight - Information

Identify Information / List Resources / Research

Identify Information

In today's internet age, the sources of information and the "how to do's" are as close as the click of a mouse or the tap on a smart phone. When I was growing up, I had to go to the library to do research. Research is to "diligently investigate." Success leaves trails. Find out what others who have achieved your goal did to succeed and do what they did. Better yet, take them to lunch and pick their brain as to how they became successful. Now we can pick up a smart phone and billions of informative web pages and videos are at our fingertips. Recently, I was grilling chicken on our barbeque. I had a tendency to overcook the chicken and my kids referred to my results as "chicken jerky." Tired of the past grilling failures, I dialed into YouTube on my smart phone – "how to grill chicken." I watched a 7-minute video and learned what do. I watched the demonstration and followed the instructions and "voila!" – we had a great chicken dinner. When I decided to become a millionaire, I studied books such as, **"Think and Grow Rich," "The Millionaire Next Door," and "The Secrets of the Millionaire Mind."** I identified books that had helped others become millionaires and followed their advice. Within a few years, I was in the "millionaire's club."

The information is out there. The sources of that information are easier than ever to access. Make a list and put it into your goals journal. Internet websites, books, audio series, seminars, trade shows, and networking are all great places to gather knowledge.

List Resources

Make a list of the information resources that you will need. If your goal is to obtain a real estate license you will need to gather the appropriate books and courses that will help you pass your test. A list of required courses will be found on your state's real estate agency website. If your goal is to obtain a bachelor's degree, make a list of the courses and requirements needed to reach that goal. Ask someone who has accomplished what you are seeking to do and find out what information and resources did they use. What books did they read? What classes did they attend? Keep a file of your findings.

Webster's defines information as "knowledge derived from study, experience, or instruction." You don't have to re-write the book. Someone has already done what you want to do (or something similar). Find that person; take their course, read their book, attend their seminar, take them to lunch. It's possible that an author may be long gone but their information is still available today. Some of the information in this book is derived from ancient writings, Webster's Dictionary, sermons, seminars, audio & video programs, and many other sources. The knowledge I gained from other sources helped propel the writing of this book.

Even more powerful than knowledge is "wisdom." Wisdom is the "right use of information & knowledge." Wisdom is the skillful use of the power of knowledge. It's doing the right thing at the right time. An ancient proverb encourages – "get wisdom, get understanding." Wisdom can be found in books written by those who have it. It is an impartation of wisdom that can be the turning point in our lives. Wisdom can be found in those with years of experience. You can save years of fruitless effort by implementing a timely word from the wise or following their system. Surround yourself with books and people who are wiser than you. Whatever you do - **get wisdom**.

## Intuition

Another source of valuable information comes from within. Your inner voice is intuition. Intuition is that quick download of information you get when making decisions or doing your research. It's your gut feeling. It's that "still, small voice" that says to you to "look at things **this** way" or simply a mental "yes" or "no" to your queries. Intuition is complimented by wisdom. When you have a download, filter it through wisdom. This will help you stay on the right course.

## Research

Once you have identified sources of wisdom and gathered information, then you need to review the knowledge and information gathered. Research once again is to "diligently investigate." Investigate comes from the root "in footsteps." You want to retrace the steps of those before you and then incorporate their successful results into your story. Learn from their failures. The great thing about learning is you don't have to repeat failures others have already gone through. Research of the heroes of success will always inspire you as they overcame failures time and time again. Keep an open mind and think outside the box when you are researching your goals. There is always something new, fresh and exciting that will come out of your investigation.

Although we want to diligently research what we need to do – don't get too bogged down in research.

Getting bogged down in research can cause procrastination, inaction, and can even cost lives. I wonder how many lives could have been saved if the newest treatment for AIDS and cancer had not gotten delayed. You need to be diligent but be careful not to over analyze.

## Windows of Opportunity

I remember when the real estate bubble began in California and other parts of the nation back in 2003 and 2004. I did my market research. I knew that there was a good chance for a correction in those markets and that it was soon to come. I also resolved through research and experience that different areas of the nation were on different real estate cycles. Central Texas was on a counter cycle to the coasts. I presented scores of seminars across the nation informing the property owners to get their over-inflated real estate equity out to safer havens such as Texas (which is on a "counter cycle"). I also knew that there was a limited time for real estate owners to take action – a "window of opportunity." Many did – but many, many more wished they had taken my advice and moved their equity out to safer havens prior to it evaporating in the real estate correction of 2007-08. As it has been said, "he who hesitates is lost." Research + wisdom + action = success.

www.PowerGoalsBook.com

Watch Video
http://bit.ly/vgqFMS

## Action Exercise

Make a list of information that you will need to gather. What books or courses will you have to take? Ask those that have a measure of success in what you are trying to do to give you their sources of wisdom. Use the internet to identify those who have accomplished what you are planning to do. See if they have written books or hold seminars. Maybe they have a mentorship or coaching program. Make a list of at least five sources that you are going to tap into to do your research. If you can come up with 10 or 20 sources, great. But start with at least five. Dedicate at least 20 minutes per day to research in your target area of expertise. Make your list:

1. _____
2. _____
3. _____
4. _____
5. _____
6. _____
7. _____
8. _____
9. _____
10. _____
11. _____
12. _____
13. _____
14. _____
15. _____
16. _____

17._____
18._____
19._____
20._____

# Identify Who'll Help
# Identify Those to Avoid
# Advocacy

Chapter IX

Step Nine – Advocates

Identify Those Who'll Help / Identify Those to Avoid / Advocacy

Identify Those Who'll Help

To reach our goals we need help. We can't do it alone. In fact, helping others get what they need is a key success factor. We help others – others help us. Zig Ziglar said, "You can have everything in life you want if you will just help enough other people get what they want." In our goals journal we need to make a list of people that will help us achieve our goal. They could be our spouse, our boss, past clients, friends, trusted advisors or a coach. What you are looking for are people whom you trust and that have your best interests in mind. You are looking for other goal oriented people who will encourage you, support your cause and back you up when the challenges come.

I co-founded a group called the "Inner Circle Business Network." This group is a number of goal oriented professionals who get together once a month to network and share ideas on success. We determined that there are wheels of relationships that are like a series of concentric circles. The goal is to bring more people who are in your "network of support" closer to your "inner circle." The circles of your group start with 5000+ people, or what we call "everybodys." They may know of you. The next circle is "acquaintances" or 500+/- people who know of you and know what you do. The next is the 70 – these are people who know you, know what you do and will refer your services willingly. They know you and trust you. Then there are "the 12." These are your close associates – your Inner Circle. Those whom you depend on and that you can **always** count on. They are close to you and will defend you at all costs. I call them **advocates** or "in relationship" doing life together with you. Then there is the inner – inner circle, the 3 +/- closest to you. I call it the "three foot rule." These are those that are within arm's length of you. You lock shields with them and they to you. As my Inner Circle friend Kenton Brown says, these are the people who would "come can get you out of a Mexican jail at 3 in the morning." Not everyone can fit in the inner – inner circle so you have to attract and choose wisely.

We need to identify those we know and those who we would like to know that can help push us towards our goals. In your goals journal, write down 12 people you know personally who could help you to reach your goal. Then write down 12 people who you would like to meet that could help you reach your goal. The key about the "would like to meet" list is not to limit yourself. I have met many of my heroes I thought I'd never personally meet, but through time I have. They were on the "list." Some of them have become personal mentors and advisors. It astonishes me and I feel blessed.

## Identify Those to Avoid

Not to sound negative but it is important to list those that you need to stay away from. It is inevitable that you will get resistance to your new idea or venture from those around you. Just know that it is part of the process. Only three percent of the world's population have written goals. So ninety-seven percent may not share your passion for achievement. Although some will support your goal, many "well meaning" people, even friends and family members may not share your dream. And then there are those who are caustic to goal achievement. Negative, pessimistic people that you need to keep at a distance.

Another group to avoid is the news media – newscasters that pour out bad news story after bad news story. You say – how will I stay informed? Don't worry about that. When it comes to the "talking heads" on TV, their information can often contain more opinions and twisted information than truth. The reason? Bad news sells better than good news. I am amazed how they can turn good news into bad news. News can become toxic to your goal achievement intentions. My wife never watches the news and she is happier and more fulfilled staying away from the "ain't it awful" broadcasts. I remember talking to her about the air crash in the Potomac about three weeks after the event. Although it had a heroic ending, my wife was unaware of the disaster. I realized she never missed the story anyway. It had no impact on her life. The news did not "take up space" in her brain.

I learned a long time ago to keep my goals **secret**. That way the well meaning "nay sayers" will not have a chance to help me change my mind. The exceptions to the rule are:

1. Other goal oriented individuals
2. Advocates who will help you get there

You want to share your dreams with those that you know, like, and trust and those who know the power of goals.

Surround yourself with positive, up-beat, goal-oriented team players. Avoid negative, energy draining, depressing, unmotivated, non-goal oriented people. They will only drag you down.

## Advocacy

"Stand by me." – Ben E. King

When striving for our goals, we need to associate with advocates. Advocate is a legal term. It means some one who you call on. Some one who will defend you and speak vehemently in favor of you. Some one who will come to your side. An advocate defends, promotes, encourages, edifies, and exhorts. The key is to find advocates and to also be an advocate. Who is it that you can call on at any time, personally and/or professionally? Who will come to your side in good times or bad? And who are *you* willing to jump up and defend or promote at any time? Anywhere?

## T.E.A.M.

In business I teach clients they need a team of advisors and advocates. The acronym I use is T.E.A.M. – Trusted Experts, Advisors & Mentors. You need to develop a team of people who will help you meet your goals. It is not hard to develop a team. Start with the professionals you already trust and ask them who they depend on for advice. Then seek to engage those individuals. The most successful professionals have a network of advocates and advisors. Connect with them and ask to become part of their network. Advocates outside of business are just as important. They could be your friend or a family member.

I know my father-in-law is an advocate to my kids because he will drop most anything to come to their side when they call on him. He will defend their cause (even at times when they are wrong). He is on their side and by their side. He is their ***advocate***.

Watch Video
http://bit.ly/vFGCpR

## Action Exercise

Make a list of your three closest advocates:

1. _____
2. _____
3. _____

Now make a commitment to contact them in the next 48 hours and tell them that they are in the inner-inner circle. Then share your goals and dreams with them and ask for them to do the same. Next, make a list of your 12 that you are "in relationship" with. Make a commitment in the next 7 days to contact your 12 and let them know how important they are and that they are an "advocate" and let them know you are an "advocate" for them. Share your dreams and goals with them and ask them to do the same. See if there is a match in your 12 that could be a match in their 12 and ask if their advocates might be a match for yours. Finally, make a written commitment to stay away from negative people and news media.

1. _____
2. _____
3. _____
4. _____
5. _____
6. _____
7. _____
8. _____

www.PowerGoalsBook.com

9. _____
10. _____
11. _____
12. _____

## Chapter X

### Step Ten – Plan

### Make a Plan / Take Action / Activation

#### Make a Plan

You will now need to make a written plan of action. Every product or mission has a plan behind. A plan of action. Every goal-achieving journey is a series of activities that are accomplished in order. A purposeful plan of action is a written "order of activities." Steps to be followed. First do "this," next do "that." If the plan is poorly written or executed, chances are it will fail. As the saying goes, "if you fail to plan, you plan to fail." I would add, "if you fail to plan well – well, you plan to fail." Think of the building of a house. The plans are set before the building is ever started. Plans need to be specific and "in order." You don't start with plumbing and electrical. Your house construction begins with clearing the lot, utility work, setting the foundation, etc. In fact, there are over 250,000 parts that go into the making of a house all of which need to be put together in a very specific order.

When you are beginning your journey you need a written plan in hand. If you don't know how to write a plan, find some one who knows how and ask them to help you. Plans can include a schematic or flow chart showing how these activities fit together. I have written step-by-step plans of action that govern my priorities and order my activities. I am also a visual person so I like to put my plans of action into a flow chart or "mind map." Think of a blueprint for building a structure. There is a very detailed schematic of the to-be-built structure. It starts with a sketch then becomes very detailed as the architect puts together the blueprints. Not a nail is driven or a brick laid without the plans laid out in visual blueprint detail prior to starting. If your goal is to start a new business you will need to have a detailed written business plan. You must know why and how your business will run and what its clear objectives are. What purpose will it serve? What problems will it solve? The business model is in the business plan. Poor planning and poor leadership are the top reasons why a majority of businesses fail in their first year. A well thought out proven business model is why franchises have a much better rate of success than mom & pop shops. If you are not sure how to put together a plan – find some one who knows how to do one and recruit them to help you with your business plan. There are courses you can take on business planning. If you are going to take a course, make sure it is from someone who has been successful. Don't waste your time learning theory from an unproven teacher. Seek wise counsel from successful people because success begets success.

When I sell a home to a customer, at our first meeting I help them make a plan for home ownership. I provide them a book I have written on home ownership. (HomeBuyingSecretsRevealed.Com) I go over the 10 steps to the home buying process. I have them write a needs & wants list. We discuss timing and financing. I then help them create a plan before we ever step into the car to go look at homes. This advance planning helps them and it helps me save time – both theirs and mine. The plan helps us stay on track. We can revise the plan as we go, but ultimately we know what we are shooting for.

When I talk with business leaders about a new venture they always ask, "What's the vision? What's the plan?" The plan does not have to be perfect nor fully complete at first, but it does need to be solid, with well thought out ideas and a definite objective. When you have your plan ready have it reviewed by several trusted advisors and advocates. Get their feedback. They can see your plan from different angles and help you "fill in the gaps."

## Priorities

Time management is putting our important primary activities on a calendar and being disciplined to perform those activities at the appointed time. This is called Time Blocking and it is crucial to goal achievement. Focused time management will accelerate you into your preferred future. It helps you stay on target and keeps you accountable to your schedule. To time block you need a weekly calendar and you "block hours" of time to do certain activities. You do this ahead of time so you can keep your weekly activities on track.

Some rules about time management:

1. Time Block your personal, family, and devotional time first.
2. Time Block your weekly primary income producing activities and guard those times ruthlessly.
3. Concentrate on the 20% of activities that give you 80% of your results
4. Set your calendar and others will line up behind you.
5. Learn how to politely yet firmly say "no" to activities that will take you off track. Saying "no" is saying "yes" to something else.
6. Learn to do what is "right." Doing good things may not necessarily be the "right" thing. Doing the "right" thing is always a good thing.

7. If you erase you must replace. If an unexpected event causes you to miss a primary activity, find another time on your calendar to replace the time you missed.

Take the First Step

I learned a long time ago about how huge taking the first step is to launch your new goal. I was at a friend's book signing and there were several people in attendance who wanted to write books. I challenged them to go home and write the first line. Write the first page. Many of them emailed me and said it was that call to action that got them moving. Simply writing one sentence. There is something very powerful about taking that first action toward your goal. Like the simple act of turning the ignition in your car. You go nowhere until you make that first simple turn of the key. Once you do you are free to move about the countryside. So take that first action at the appointed time. And that time may be right now. **Now** is better than later. **Now** has power. **Now** creates momentum. So if your goal is to write down your goals, do it today. Use your goals journal and ***start today***. Procrastination is a dream killer. Busyness is a modern plague. You must not succumb to all the other voices calling for your attention. So what is it going to be – today? Someday? Or never? A respected author I met told me that the wealthiest place on earth is the cemetery. Why? Because there were so many books, songs, businesses, etc, that could have been created but people took them to the sweet bye-and-bye. They never started what they were originally destined to accomplish. Don't be like those who bury their dreams and aspirations. You are blessed to be a blessing. Make a plan and get started, and if possible, start today!

## Taking Your Goal Into an Action Plan

Achieving any big goal is a series of small goals. The best way to eat an elephant is one bite at a time. Maybe your three-year goal is to triple your income or to lose 20 pounds. Divide the goal by 3 and that will tell you how much you will have to work towards each year to meet your goal. For instance, if you currently make $3000 per month and you want to make $9000 per month, you will need to increase your income producing activities to make an additional $2000 per month by year-end. Then by the end of the second year, another $2000 per month and by year three another $2000 per month. This will put you at the $9000 income figure. Now take the additional $2000 per month figure and break it down by week. There are roughly four weeks in a month which equates to $500 per week. What income producing activities will you have to do to make an extra $500 per week? I can think of a few. One of mine is – get up an hour or two earlier. Another may be to add a second job, do network marketing, or better yet, get more productive at your current job so you can get a raise (or all of the above). What if your goal is weight loss? To lose 20 pounds over 36 months is a little over half a pound per month or 1/8 of a pound per week. What amount of exercise will you have to do and what kind of foods will you have to cut out to lose 1/8 of a pound per week? What will you have to add to your daily routine to meet your goal's objectives? What will you have to cut out of your routine to help you reach your goal?

Goal achievement is not about doing so much as it is about "becoming." What kind of person will you have to become to reach your goal? The big how is reached by a series of little hows. So once you have decided on reaching your big dream you will have to break it down into smaller goals and then break it down to your weekly and daily activities.

I start with the end goal in mind and then back out my timeline from the end to the beginning. I have to do lists that are spread out in columns where I can categorize my activities based on the timing for their completion. Think about your projects the way you would plan a wedding. You have to work backwards from the "date." My to do lists are broken down into what I have to do over specific periods of time. Start with the end and work backwards.

## Activation

I love the multiple definitions for activation because they are so descriptive and motivating. Having a goal backed by a solid plan of action and then getting started is a recipe for success. Once you have this recipe, you must then light a fire and get cookin'. You must **activate** your goal. Webster's defines activate as – to "set in motion."

Like the gun going off at the start of the big race – BANG! – everyone gets moving. To *activate* is also a military term – to gather and organize the troops for a mission. When you activate you will be surprised how your crew, your cohorts, your staff, get moving. Activation also means to mix with oxygen. Mix your dreams and goals with life giving oxygen. When you activate, you breathe life into your goal – you become *inspired*.

Activation is also a term used to describe *purification*. When you see the fountain running in a pond of stagnant water, it is activating and purifying the water. It is getting the water in motion adding life-giving oxygen to the pond. If your season in life feels a little stagnant, you may just need some life-giving activation.

Activation also means to accelerate a reaction as with heat. When you start the fire beneath that pot of water, it is relatively calm. Give it 15 minutes on high heat and it is activated into a wild boil. Taking that first action will light the fire under your goal.

In science, to activate a substance is to make it radioactive. Part of the process in making the atomic bomb includes turning water into heavy water through activation. Your dreams and goals can become a nuclear chain reaction leading to massive releases of energy. Do you want that kind of explosive release of energy? I do! Get ready, get set – *get Activated*!

www.PowerGoalsBook.com

Watch Video
http://bit.ly/vxmFab

## Action Exercise

In your goals journal, make a simple 10 bullet point plan of action for how you are going to accomplish your goal.

1. _____
2. _____
3. _____
4. _____
5. _____
6. _____
7. _____
8. _____
9. _____
10. _____

Next, list the first simple step you are going to take in the next 48 hours to activate your goal. Then take that action and say to yourself, "activation has begun...so be it."

## Action Plan

Things I have to do in the next:

A) 1-3 Days
B) 3-10 Days
C) 10-30 Days
D) 60-90 Days
E) 3 months, 6 months, 12 months, 36 months

www.PowerGoalsBook.com

    Place your goal at the end of its timeline and then work backwards. What will have to happen at each phase of the way over time? This will give you a priority list of the things you will have to work on for the week, the month, the quarter, etc. It is a list that is re-written time and time again as you get closer to your deadline. You will find great satisfaction as you cross off your smaller accomplishments along the way. For example, my book writing 1-year plan may look like this:

| A) 1-3 | B) 3-10 | C) 10-30 | D) 30-90 | E) 3 mo–1 yr |
|---|---|---|---|---|
| Topic – Purpose | Outline Completed | Time Block Two hours writing per day | Continue writing | Published book |
| Goal Setting Exercise | Chapter Bullet Points Itemized | | Manuscript completed | Promotion |
| Activation | | | Editor & graphic artist engaged | Distribution |
| Begin | | | Cover design completed | |

## Action Exercise

Take a one-year goal and put it into a plan of action timeline exercise like I have done with my book example.

| A) 1-3 | B) 3-10 | C) 10-30 | D) 30-90 | E) 3 mo–1 yr |
|--------|---------|----------|----------|--------------|
| _____ | _____ | _____ | _____ | _____ |
| _____ | _____ | _____ | _____ | _____ |
| _____ | _____ | _____ | _____ | _____ |
| _____ | _____ | _____ | _____ | _____ |
| _____ | _____ | _____ | _____ | _____ |
| _____ | _____ | _____ | _____ | _____ |
| _____ | _____ | _____ | _____ | _____ |
| _____ | _____ | _____ | _____ | _____ |
| _____ | _____ | _____ | _____ | _____ |
| _____ | _____ | _____ | _____ | _____ |
| _____ | _____ | _____ | _____ | _____ |
| _____ | _____ | _____ | _____ | _____ |

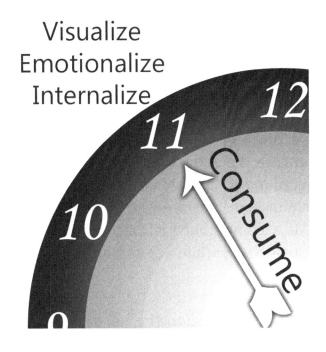

## Chapter XI

### Step Eleven – Consume

### Visualize / Emotionalize / Internalize

#### Visualize

Now take time to get in a quiet place and close your eyes and visualize your goal – as completed. Visualization is very inspiring and motivating. A habit of visualizing your goal "as completed" will keep the wind in your sails.

Make a habit of visualizing your preferred future – constantly. Why? Because there are so many visuals competing for our mind's eye. You want *your* visuals at the forefront of your consciousness, not some one else's. Advertisers know this strategy all to well. Just last night I was watching a show and it seemed like every commercial was of hot, steamy pizza. The visual of melting cheese, pepperoni, mmmmm. It was so visually compelling that I could even smell the pizza. Guess what ended up in the oven before the show was over. Yep, a pizza. The visuals prompted me to take action. You need to keep the visuals of your dream constantly on your mind. Visualize your goal "as accomplished" all of the time. Either we control the visuals that parade across our mind or something else will.

We must develop the habit of becoming a destiny visionary. Many years ago, I remember a motivational trainer came to my office and told me to find a picture of one of my goals – such as a dream vacation or a fancy car. Then he told me to cut it out and glue a photo of myself into the photo. Then keep it in a place where I could see it daily. It worked! My photo was of Ka'anapali Beach in Maui and I put a photo of myself and my future wife in the picture and sure enough within a year that dream trip happened. That same amazing power of visualization happened later when we planned our dream home. I sketched the downstairs and upstairs of my dream home. My wife could "see" it in her mind's eye but was not a good sketcher. Nonetheless she could see it. She described the "living room over looking the pool with a beautiful lake view below." Not more than four years after drawing and dreaming we found that home. Or should I say – the home found us. "Out of the blue" a division president for a large homebuilder called me and we talked shop for a while until he mentioned his new home was nearing completion. I asked him what he was going to do with his old home. He said that he was going to put it on the market but not until he moved into his new one. He described his current home to me and I said, "That sounds like a property we may be interested in." Of course, it was nearly exactly what my wife and I had visualized years before. Specifically – the downstairs was almost exactly what I had sketched out. And yes, it has a pool and gorgeous lake view. Needless to say our family enjoys the dream home. If we never visualized it we may have hesitated or not recognized it when the opportunity came to us. The funny thing is that the home was never on the open market.

## Emotionalize

We are "feeling" people. Most of what we do is an attempt to create a "feeling" or an emotion that leads to joy and pleasure. We try to avoid and move away from things that are negative, painful, and sorrowful. It's our nature. In goal coaching, I ask:

1. What is it that you want?
2. Why do you want it?
3. What will it do for you?
4. How will it make you *feel*?

If the goal is to open up an orphanage in Costa Rica it would be accompanied by the ultimate feeling associated with that goal being accomplished. "Wow, I feel great. Several dozen children now have food, clothing, shelter, education, and a future because of the goal being accomplished. What a good feeling." We can attempt to think ourselves to success but the ultimate driving factor is how we *feel* about the success. If we have heard growing up "You won't amount to anything" or "money is the root of all evil," you may have been improperly programmed and you might have to "clear the hard drive," reformat, reboot. We all have a common desire to be happy, healthy, and prosperous. No one wants to be depressed, unhealthy, and broke. Unfortunately, too many go through life in mediocrity because of limiting emotional baggage from the past. Old, negative baggage is a curse and needs to be dumped. I am no therapist, but if you need one, go for it. Get help. Go to counseling. Whatever you do, don't let past hang-ups keep you from moving forward.

So much of our activities are directed by how we feel. So we must associate positive feelings to the priorities that will move us towards our objective and attach negative feelings to things that hold us back or get us off track. By no means should we become negative people. Just push away those negative activities that create a negative mindset. One negative activity to avoid is complaining. Complaining is like a garbage magnet. Refrain from complaining – it doesn't help anyway.

Emotionalization is a heart phenomenon. When you attach wonderful feelings to your preferred outcome, you create positive anticipation, excitement, and drive. Listen to positive, upbeat music. Watch encouraging videos and listen to motivational programs. Do positive affirmations every day can help keep a positive emotional base. Keep repeating the good results that come your way. No matter the circumstance, keep applying positive affirmations. Short sentences repeated over and over. A little rhyme to the affirmation like – "I am happy and healthy in every way, I am getting better and better every day." One of my heroes encourages me saying "whatever is true, whatever is noble, whatever is right, whatever is pure, whatever is lovely, whatever is admirable – if anything is excellent or praiseworthy – think about such things."

Attach the deepest emotion – "love" – to your activities. "I love what I am doing and where I am going." I love helping others. I emotionalized writing this book because I know it would help others.

Another awesome emotion to tie your goal to is gratitude. Be thankful that you are headed towards a wonderful preferred future. Will there be setbacks and disappointments along the way? Yes, but they should only serve to make you more grateful when you overcome them. Become a grateful overcomer and enjoy the journey.

You need to emotionalize the goal as achieved – similar to visualizing, take a moment to imagine & feel the experience as it will be in the future.

## Internalize

Next you need to internalize your goal. This goes beyond visualization and emotionalization. This is where you actually swallow your goal. You eat it whole so to speak. Making it a part of you. You are not going to eat anything that is something you are not committed to. Are you willing to internalize your goal? Your goal then must become a part of you. It becomes part of your identity. You are what you eat, right? Consume worthwhile, passionate, exciting goals, and you will be feeding on the fruit of a successful, preferred future.

When you get that dream in your stomach, you can feel it. You carry it wherever you go. The goal is now nourishment & sustenance to your progress, rooted deep inside you – in your gut. Ancient texts speak of a man who was told to deliver an important message to an entire nation that needed help. He was told to "eat this scroll I am giving you, fill your stomach with it!" When he ate it, he said it tasted like honey in his mouth. You must want your goal so bad that you can taste it. A dream fulfilled is as sweet as honey – "taste and see."

Another way to internalize is by breathing in your goal. When you contemplate your goal achieved, take a slow, deep breath through your nose. Hold your breath while you focus on your goal. Then breathe out a satisfied exhale through your mouth. When you inhale you are energizing your blood. You are invigorating and inspiring yourself. When you breathe in, whisper, "I receive this."

Then breathe out slowly like a sigh of relief and as you do speak the words "it shall be so..."

## Mind, Heart, Gut

When you visualize your goal, you see it (and hear it). This is a mind thing. A mental event. When you emotionalize your goal, this is a heart thing – a feeling event. When you internalize your goal, this is a gut thing. It becomes almost instinctual. When you align the mind, the heart, and the gut with your goal, you have created an incredible twain that will propel you and sustain you towards your accomplishment.

Watch Video
http://bit.ly/uSuZhG

Action Exercise

Now take your written goal and put it in front of you. Read it aloud and put your hand on your head, close your eyes, "visualize" your goal, and say "___(goal)___" – "so shall it be." Then put your hand on your heart and "emotionalize" your goal and follow with the words – "so shall it be." Then put your hand on your belly and "consume" your goal and again finish with "so shall it be." You have anchored yourself to your goal and have deemed it "done." Repeat this process every day. It only takes a few minutes and it will change your life.

## Chapter XII

### Step Twelve – Power

### Persistence / Patience / Prayer

#### Persistence

Throughout your journey towards your goal, you must **commit to** and **persist** until it comes to fruition. You must have a "never give up" attitude. You must press in and press on towards the accomplishment. Any worthwhile achievement will meet resistance. If goal achievement were easy everyone would do it. Remember, only 3% of us take the time to even write our goals. It does take work and it does take persistence. There will be times of struggle and times of breakthrough. One thing is for sure; you can't win unless you stay in the game. Yes, it may take longer and take more sweat than you originally signed up for, but if you persist and persevere you will make it to the finish line. In my business I have never had a case where a client who really wanted to own a home could not get one as long as they did what was necessary and **persisted**. It's true; I worked with one client for three years to get her a home. Credit, divorce, and job issues all came into play, but she never gave up and I never gave up on her. Now she is a happy home owner. Unfortunately, I have also had clients who gave up. They quit. I doubt they are home owners today and they may rent forever. But after thousands of transactions and nearly thirty years in real estate, all who persisted got their home.

Persistence builds character and confidence. It prepares us to push through the resistance during the tough times. It builds our strength to accomplish even greater goals in the future. The greater the goal the greater the need for persistence. One of my heroes stated, "...one thing I do, forgetting what is behind and reaching forward to those things which are ahead, I press toward the goal – for the prize..." The root of the word persistence means, "stand firm." If your goal is worthwhile enough you must make a stand for the cause. "Stand your ground!" Too many quit when the going gets tough. Don't be a quitter. You may have to make a detour along the way, but keep moving forward. My encouragement to you is to press on my friend, press on.

## Patience

Ahhh, patience. A word that my triple Type A personality does not grasp well. My mind says "I want my goal and I want it now." Over the years I have learned a measure of patience. Although I am certainly not the poster child of patience, most of my advocates would agree I now have more peace and patience than I had in the past. And patience is crucial to the goal accomplishment journey. Patience helps create humility. Humility helps build patience. If we could have it "all" *right now* – anything – any time, we would become spoiled brats and be diminished by it. Our drive to succeed would be compromised. I have learned to "smell the flowers along the way." Learning patience helps us in our journey and in our relationships. Do you feel uncomfortable standing in the grocery line with an impatient person? I know I used to be that disquieting person tapping his toe and doing the heavy sigh – until I moved to Texas from California. In California, everything moved faster, cars go 90 miles per hour on the freeway. The Starbucks line moves quicker; no one has time to smell coffee or the roses. You just might get pushed in line from behind or pushed off the freeway by a Porsche or a soccer mom in a minivan. In Texas the culture is more friendly, easy going and talkative. This led to longer waits in line and slower traffic. Impatient people don't take time to smell flowers. They miss the joy and pleasure of being like a child? To dance and play like children along the way. Needless to say I had to learn patience and I am far better off by learning the art of patience. I remember thinking "either Texas needs to change or I am going to have to change" (or go crazy). I decided to change.

I can honestly say that every goal I have "gone for" took longer and cost more in terms of effort and resources than I first considered. Patience and persistence pulled me through. You must learn and develop the art of patience. It is crucial to keep you from becoming disappointed and discouraged.

Patience gives you peace. Peace during the inevitable setbacks. Peace during the storms. It was said, "peace…which surpasses all understanding will guard your hearts and minds…." Peace guards us and protects us. Patience gives us a peaceful confident expectation that a preferred future will come to pass. Show me someone without patience and I will show you someone without peace. Patience is a virtue and when tied together with persistence it creates an incredible force in our lives.

### Prayer

As we come to the final section of power goals, I congratulate you for making it this far. Statistically, a majority of books that people start to read are never finished. I admit some books that I start to read I never finish. Either I lose interest or another book comes along. Or my wife decides she likes the one I am reading and begins reading it herself and then I can't find it. So I thank you for making it to this point and coming to the final and most important section of this book. The ultimate key to unlocking the power of goals. The catalyst and the sustainer of your goals journey. The secret to most all great achievement – the power of *prayer*. I know – you are saying, "come on, I didn't move through this process just to get to a dissertation on religious practices." Believe me, this is not about religiosity; it is about the key to ultimate success. It's about your prayers being answered and dreams being achieved, and that's a good thing.

Although I am no expert on this subject, I am a firm believer in the power of prayer in goal achievement. My belief in prayer comes from "results." From fulfillment of my desires and dreams. **Power goals are a result of power prayers**. Prayer should be the beginning and the ending of the goal setting practice. Prayer should saturate the process along the way. I started this book with step one – Want – decide / desire / commit but before this first step should be prayer. Why did I not begin the book with prayer? Because people might think I am "preachy" – that is not my intention. What I do know is what works and that is why I am sharing prayer with you. In fact, I saturate the whole goal setting process in prayer, meditation, and reflection. Prayer is "to make entreaty," an "earnest request." To who? The Creator of the Universe. To the Intelligence behind existence – God!

In His Word he said, "You have not because you ask not." I learned a long time ago "if you don't ask – you don't get." Learn to speak out your desired result and to seek revelation from beyond our own limited space and time. When I pray I am thankful that my goal has already been achieved. Where? At it's designated time in the future. In prayer, I often get perfect solutions to a problem or a new direction to move in that I had not considered. Sometimes in prayer I get a great idea, or a song, or a cool "vision." When you lift up your goals in prayer, you are presenting your goals to the invisible and un-manifested realm and you are asking God to make them visible - to make them reality. True prayer brings peace, a peace that surpasses understanding. Along with prayer I encourage you to meditate on your goal. One definition of meditation is to "revolve around in one's mind." When you meditate on something, you are looking at it from all different angles. I am not talking about the secluded mountaintop guru type of meditation. I am talking about rotating your objective around in your mind's eye with an expectant, prayerful, supernatural perspective.

Finally, I encourage you in prayer to come from a position of thanksgiving. The powerful combination of prayer, meditation and thanksgiving will create an atmosphere of positive expectation and results. Gratitude is a most powerful force. Sometimes a simple "thank you" can open doors of opportunity that otherwise would not open. Thanks giving is ingrained in our nature. We all love to give and receive thanks. So thank you! Thank you for reading my book. I hope it has helped you on this journey we call life. My hope for you is a life of setting and achieving goals. My prayer for you is, "may your goals and dreams come true and you receive a life full of love, joy,

www.PowerGoalsBook.com

peace, health, and prosperity." God bless you! See you at the top!

Watch Video
http://bit.ly/vmbTyG

Action Exercise

Write your goal now as accomplished. Put a circle around it. Now put your finger on it and say out loud "I commit to this purpose and will persist until it becomes real." Now close your eyes and say, "I will enjoy the process and have peace and patience along the journey. Now say to yourself that "my prayer is that God grant me this goal as an inheritance of the dream you planted inside of me. Thank you."

## Review

Take time each week to review your goals and to run through the twelve steps. It only takes 15 minutes. A habit of reviewing will help you stay on track. Pick a goals accountability partner and share your goals journey with them. Get together once a month or at least once per quarter and review each other's goals. Find a networking group or start one that is success oriented. Hang out with goal-oriented people. Do life together. Encourage and edify one another. Do these things and it will change your life. My encouragement to you is to live, love, and grow in the purposes that God has for you and to help others do the same.

www.PowerGoalsBook.com

www.PowerGoalsBook.com

# Action Exercises, Consolidated

Chapter I – Step One – Want (Desire / Decide / Commit)

Reflection

Make a list of goals you already have accomplished. It is important to pat yourself on the back for your past successes:

_____
_____
_____
_____
_____

What accomplishments or endeavors are you thankful for and proud of?

_____
_____
_____
_____
_____

Who have you met or become in relationship with that you are thankful for?

_____
_____
_____
_____
_____

What **one** accomplishment or endeavor are you most proud of?

_____
_____
_____
_____
_____

What events had the most positive impact on your life?

_____
_____
_____
_____
_____

If you had to do it all over again, what experience would you like to re-live again?

_____
_____
_____
_____
_____

## Projection

Now to get your creative ambition juices flowing, answer this question: If you were handed $3 million, tax free, what would you choose to do with your time? What activities would you pursue? How would your day look?

Where would you live? What kind of car would you drive? With whom would you spend your time?

_____
_____
_____
_____
_____

If you had exactly one year to live from today, what would you do with your time? With whom would you spend time? What activities would you pursue?

_____
_____
_____
_____
_____

10-Minute Life Changing Goal Setting Exercise:

Get in a quiet place without distractions. Get a timer or stopwatch. Close your eyes and imagine you had unlimited funds and you were free from any hindering responsibilities. If you could have anything you want in the next three years, what would it be? Now list all things you want for yourself, your family, your community, your finances, relationships you want to have, spiritual desires, and material things. Remember, no limitations – make a list. You have 3 minutes:

1. _____
2. _____

3. _____
4. _____
5. _____
6. _____
7. _____
8. _____
9. _____
10. _____
11. _____
12. _____
13. _____
14. _____
15. _____
16. _____
17. _____
18. _____
19. _____
20. _____

(If you have more than 20, keep going!)

Now circle the **three** items that if achieved would have the biggest positive impact on your life. Then out of those three, pick the one goal that would have the biggest impact on your life. This is the goal that we are going to use throughout the action exercises in this book.

You will be amazed that 2/3rd of your 3 year written goals will be accomplished in the first 12 to 18 months. You have begun the journey. Now let's go to work.

Chapter II – Step Two – Know (Believe / Faith / Know)

From chapter one's goal exercise, take your #1 goal (and the others when you are ready). Put your left index finger on that #1 goal and your right hand on your forehead and say "I have this" or "I am this" and follow with "so be it." Say I believe  (Goal)  to be true – so be it. Now move your right hand to your heart and repeat, "I have this or I am this, so be it," then to your stomach and repeat it again followed by "so be it." Then open your eyes and say, "I receive it."

## Chapter III – Step Three – Ink (Write It / Speak It / Proclaim It)

Take your important goals from the chapter one exercise and fill in these sentences – put the goal in present tense (as completed):

I am _____
(Identity / Existence)
Because _____
(Reason / Cause)
So that _____
(Results / Effect)

Example:   I am earning twenty thousand per month every month by June
Because I have children going to college and I want a nicer home
So that I am comfortably providing for my family's security and college education.

Repeat this exercise with all your important goals and keep them in your goals journal. Put the statements in a place you can see them daily. On your bathroom mirror, a white board at your office, or on the visor of your car.

www.PowerGoalsBook.com

## Chapter IV – Step Four – Motives (List Benefits / List Consequences / Motivations

List ten to twenty benefits you or others will expect to enjoy when you reach your goal. The first ten will be easy. It will get more difficult as you get to twenty. Push through - the more benefits you list, the more motivated you will be.

1. _____
2. _____
3. _____
4. _____
5. _____
6. _____
7. _____
8. _____
9. _____
10. _____
11. _____
12. _____
13. _____
14. _____
15. _____
16. _____
17. _____
18. _____
19. _____
20. _____

List five or more serious consequences that will result if you do not reach your goal. Be real. These may be your catalyst for change.

1. _____
2. _____
3. _____
4. _____
5. _____

Anchoring Exercise

Now close your eyes, think of your goal, and open your hands as if to receive a gift. Say, "I receive the benefits of my goal achieved." Next, put your hands out in front of you as if to push away something you didn't want and say, "I resist the notion of my goal not being achieved. I push away the consequences." Now raise your hands above your head and say, "I reach into the future and pull my goal to me." Then pull your hands down towards your heart as if pulling fruit off of a tree. Then say, "I receive, I believe – so be it."

## Chapter V – Step Five – Boundaries (Analyze Starting Point / Define Completion / Boundaries)

### Analyze Starting Point

For each of your goals, write down your current starting position. For instance, if your goal is to have $1 million cash by age 55, write down how much cash you have right now. If you are trying to achieve a certain weight, write down your current weight.

Where are you currently?

_____

Now clearly define your goal as completed:

_____

# Chapter VI – Step Six – Time (Set a Deadline / Set a Starting Date / The Stopwatch)

Now take your most desired goal and write down a start date:

I will begin _____
                             (goal)
on  _____.
                          (start date)

Now write down a deadline. Use a future date in the present tense, Ex. "I weigh __X__ pounds on June 1, 2014":

_____
                             (goal)
_____.
                     (completion date)

Now read the goal and the start date and deadline aloud so you hear it for yourself.

## Chapter VII – Step Seven – Survey (List Obstacles / Identify Opportunities / Survey Terrain)

List five opportunities that you can think of that currently align with your goal that you can capitalize on:

1. _____
2. _____
3. _____
4. _____
5. _____

Circle the best opportunity for you at this time. Now say out loud, "I will seize this opportunity now."

List the 3 biggest obstacles or fears you have that would hold you back from obtaining your goal.

1. _____
2. _____
3. _____

Now declare out loud these obstacles as small, not significant, and having no power over your destiny.

# Chapter VIII – Step Eight – Information (Identify Information / List Resources / Research)

Make a list of information that you will need to gather. What books or courses will you have to take? Ask those that have a measure of success in what you are trying to do to give you their sources of wisdom. Use the internet to identify those who have accomplished what you are planning to do. See if they have written books or hold seminars. Maybe they have a mentorship or coaching program. Make a list of at least five sources that you are going to tap into to do your research. If you can come up with 10 or 20 sources, great. But start with at least five. Dedicate at least 20 minutes per day to research in your target area of expertise. Make your list:

1. _____
2. _____
3. _____
4. _____
5. _____
6. _____
7. _____
8. _____
9. _____
10. _____
11. _____
12. _____
13. _____
14. _____
15. _____

16._____
17._____
18._____
19._____
20._____

# Chapter IX – Step Nine – Advocates (Identify Those Who'll Help / Identify Those to Avoid / Advocacy)

Make a list of your three closest advocates:

1. _____
2. _____
3. _____

Now make a commitment to contact them in the next 48 hours and tell them that they are in the inner-inner circle. Then share your goals and dreams with them and ask for them to do the same. Next, make a list of your 12 that you are "in relationship" with. Make a commitment in the next 7 days to contact your 12 and let them know how important they are and that they are an "advocate" and let them know you are an "advocate" for them. Share your dreams and goals with them and ask them to do the same. See if there is a match in your 12 that could be a match in their 12 and ask if their advocates might be a match for yours. Finally, make a written commitment to stay away from negative people and news media.

1. _____
2. _____
3. _____
4. _____
5. _____
6. _____
7. _____

8. _____
9. _____
10. _____
11. _____
12. _____

## Chapter X – Step Ten – Plan (Make a Plan / Take Action / Activation)

In your goals journal, make a simple 10 bullet point plan of action or how you are going to accomplish your goal.

1. _____
2. _____
3. _____
4. _____
5. _____
6. _____
7. _____
8. _____
9. _____
10. _____

Next, list the first simple step you are going to take in the next 48 hours to activate your goal. Then take that action and say to yourself, "activation has begun…so be it."

www.PowerGoalsBook.com

## Action Plan

Make a one-year goal and goal and put it into a plan of action timeline exercise like I have done with my book example.

| A) 1-3 | B) 3-10 | C) 10-30 | D) 30-90 | E) 3 mo–1 yr |
|--------|---------|----------|----------|--------------|
| _____ | _____ | _____ | _____ | _____ |
| _____ | _____ | _____ | _____ | _____ |
| _____ | _____ | _____ | _____ | _____ |
| _____ | _____ | _____ | _____ | _____ |
| _____ | _____ | _____ | _____ | _____ |
| _____ | _____ | _____ | _____ | _____ |
| _____ | _____ | _____ | _____ | _____ |
| _____ | _____ | _____ | _____ | _____ |
| _____ | _____ | _____ | _____ | _____ |
| _____ | _____ | _____ | _____ | _____ |
| _____ | _____ | _____ | _____ | _____ |
| _____ | _____ | _____ | _____ | _____ |

# Chapter XI – Step Eleven – Consume (Visualize / Emotionalize / Internalize)

Now take your written goal and put it in front of you. Read it aloud and put your hand on your head, close your eyes, and say "_____" – "so shall it be." Then put your hand on your heart and repeat your goal and follow with the words – "so shall it be." Then put your hand on your belly and repeat the goal and again finish with "so shall it be." You have anchored yourself to your goal and have deemed it "done." Repeat this process every day. It only takes a few minutes and it will change your life.

## Chapter XII – Step Twelve – Power (Persistence / Patience / Prayer)

Write your goal now as accomplished. Put a circle around it. Now put your finger on it and say out loud "I commit to this purpose and will persist until it becomes real." Now close your eyes and say, "I will enjoy the process and have peace and patience along the journey. Now say to yourself that "my prayer is that God grant me this goal as an inheritance of the dream you planted inside of me. Thank you."

www.PowerGoalsBook.com

## About the Author

Kenn Renner is a national speaker, author, investor, and entrepreneur. He has closed over $250 million in sales as a top producing real estate broker. He created the #1 ranked YouTube channel for real estate nationwide. He has produced a multitude of educational and motivational programs including seminars, television shows, music CDs, books, DVDs, video & audio programs. Kenn resides in Austin, TX with his wife Michele and his children Justin, Christine, and Julia. He enjoys songwriting, travel, golf, and wintersports.

## Many Thanks too...

Thanks to all who helped and encouraged me to get this book written. If I missed anyone please forgive me and you have my thanks anyway. My wife Michele, my family, George & Faye Walter and the rest of the Walter family, Daniel Sanford, Stephanie McCord, Mary Lewis, Tracy Seeber, Kenton Brown, Phyllis Blackwell, Rob Hutton, Joshua & Tiffany Geary, Scott Carley, Dominik Kilpatrick, Danny Thompson, Ben Kinney, Dr. Raymond Larson, Wesley Young, Debbie De Grote, Rick Ebert, Mark Loper, Eddie & Alice Smith, Ras & Bev Robinson, Mary Lynne Gibbs, Dianna Kokoszka, Tony DiCello, J.P. Lewis, Mo Andersen, Cary Sylvester, Jay Papasan, & all the rest at the Keller Williams International office and most of all Jesus.

For additional programs, audio, DVD, video, and additional copies of the book (bulk pricing), go to:

www.PowerGoalsBook.com

CPSIA information can be obtained at www.ICGtesting.com
Printed in the USA
LVOW011915080313

323413LV00022B/854/P

9 781466 468825